Current
CONTROVERSIES

Poverty and
Homelessness

Other Books in the Current Controversies Series

Poverty and Homelessness

Noël Merino, Book Editor

GREENHAVEN PRESS
A part of Gale, Cengage Learning

GALE
CENGAGE Learning·

Farmington Hills, Mich • San Francisco • New York • Waterville, Maine
Meriden, Conn • Mason, Ohio • Chicago

Elizabeth Des Chenes, *Director, Content Strategy*
Cynthia Sanner, *Publisher*
Douglas Dentino, *Manager, New Product*

© 2014 Greenhaven Press, a part of Gale, Cengage Learning

WCN: 01-100-101

Gale and Greenhaven Press are registered trademarks used herein under license.

For more information, contact:
Greenhaven Press
27500 Drake Rd.
Farmington Hills, MI 48331-3535
Or you can visit our Internet site at gale.cengage.com

For product information and technology assistance, contact us at

Gale Customer Support, 1-800-877-4253
For permission to use material from this text or product, submit all requests online at
www.cengage.com/permissions

Further permissions questions can be emailed to permissionrequest@cengage.com

Articles in Greenhaven Press anthologies are often edited for length to meet page requirements. In addition, original titles of these works are changed to clearly present the main thesis and to explicitly indicate the author's opinion. Every effort is made to ensure that Greenhaven Press accurately reflects the original intent of the authors. Every effort has been made to trace the owners of copyrighted material.

Cover image copyright © Jon Le-Bon/Shutterstock.com.

LIBRARY OF CONGRESS CATALOGING-IN-PUBLICATION DATA

Poverty and homelessness / Noël Merino, book editor.
     pages cm. -- (Current controversies)
     Includes bibliographical references and index.
     ISBN 978-0-7377-6886-2 (hardcover) -- ISBN 978-0-7377-6887-9 (pbk.)
     1. Homelessness--United States. 2. Poverty--United States. 3. Homelessness--Government policy--United States. 4. Poverty--Government policy--United States. I. Merino, Noël, editor of compilation.
     HV4505.P6792 2014
     362.50973--dc23
                                                                                2013027889

Printed in the United States of America
1 2 3 4 5 6 7 18 17 16 15 14

Contents

Despite evidence of a housing crisis, the government has responded by cutting the federal housing budget and supporting a questionable new approach that targets subpopulations of the homeless, such as military veterans, and offers little else to the remaining 3.5 million people who lack access to affordable housing.

No: Poverty and Homelessness Are Not Serious Problems

Chapter 2: Do Government Social Assistance Programs Help the Poor?

The number of Americans eligible for benefits and the number of people claiming benefits under the Supplemental Nutrition Assistance Program has increased significantly since 2007, the start of the Great Recession, and is forecast to continue to rise until 2014.

Yes: Government Social Assistance Programs Help the Poor

No: Government Social Assistance Programs Do Not Help the Poor

Despite increased government spending on welfare programs in recent years, poverty has not been reduced. This is because the focus of our current anti-poverty system is on making the poor more comfortable, rather than on creating the conditions that will help people escape poverty. As such, we need a new approach to fighting poverty that emphasizes the free market and not government handouts to the poor.

Chapter 3: How Should Poverty in America Be Addressed?

Increasing inequality in America has led to favoritism for the rich and increasing poverty and lack of opportunity for everyone else. Such inequality not only hurts those at the bottom of the economic ladder but also stifles growth and produces inefficiencies in the country's free-market system.

The biggest cause of poverty in America is children born outside of marriage to less-educated parents. Whereas in the top third of income earners in the country children are raised by married, educated couples, in the bottom third more children are born out of wedlock and raised by a single mother with only a high school education. And these children are roughly five times as likely to be poor as those born to married parents. As such, the best way to reduce poverty is to encourage marriage among young adults.

Chapter 4: What Strategies Would Benefit the Homeless in America?

Federal low-income assistance programs have been cut at a time when they are needed most, putting more people at risk of homelessness and poverty. The US government needs to increase funding for housing assistance, especially in the area of housing vouchers for low-income individuals and families, since these investments, while costly, will pay dividends in reducing poverty and homelessness.

Foreword

By definition, controversies are "discussions of questions in which opposing opinions clash" (*Webster's Twentieth Century Dictionary Unabridged*). Few would deny that controversies are a pervasive part of the human condition and exist on virtually every level of human enterprise. Controversies transpire between individuals and among groups, within nations and between nations. Controversies supply the grist necessary for progress by providing challenges and challengers to the status quo. They also create atmospheres where strife and warfare can flourish. A world without controversies would be a peaceful world; but it also would be, by and large, static and prosaic.

The Series' Purpose

The purpose of the Current Controversies series is to explore many of the social, political, and economic controversies dominating the national and international scenes today. Titles selected for inclusion in the series are highly focused and specific. For example, from the larger category of criminal justice, Current Controversies deals with specific topics such as police brutality, gun control, white collar crime, and others. The debates in Current Controversies also are presented in a useful, timeless fashion. Articles and book excerpts included in each title are selected if they contribute valuable, long-range ideas to the overall debate. And wherever possible, current information is enhanced with historical documents and other relevant materials. Thus, while individual titles are current in focus, every effort is made to ensure that they will not become quickly outdated. Books in the Current Controversies series will remain important resources for librarians, teachers, and students for many years.

In addition to keeping the titles focused and specific, great care is taken in the editorial format of each book in the series. Book introductions and chapter prefaces are offered to provide background material for readers. Chapters are organized around several key questions that are answered with diverse opinions representing all points on the political spectrum. Materials in each chapter include opinions in which authors clearly disagree as well as alternative opinions in which authors may agree on a broader issue but disagree on the possible solutions. In this way, the content of each volume in Current Controversies mirrors the mosaic of opinions encountered in society. Readers will quickly realize that there are many viable answers to these complex issues. By questioning each author's conclusions, students and casual readers can begin to develop the critical thinking skills so important to evaluating opinionated material.

Current Controversies is also ideal for controlled research. Each anthology in the series is composed of primary sources taken from a wide gamut of informational categories including periodicals, newspapers, books, US and foreign government documents, and the publications of private and public organizations. Readers will find factual support for reports, debates, and research papers covering all areas of important issues. In addition, an annotated table of contents, an index, a book and periodical bibliography, and a list of organizations to contact are included in each book to expedite further research.

Perhaps more than ever before in history, people are confronted with diverse and contradictory information. During the Persian Gulf War, for example, the public was not only treated to minute-to-minute coverage of the war, it was also inundated with critiques of the coverage and countless analyses of the factors motivating US involvement. Being able to sort through the plethora of opinions accompanying today's major issues, and to draw one's own conclusions, can be a complicated and frustrating struggle. It is the editors' hope that Current Controversies will help readers with this struggle.

Introduction

"An inaccurate poverty measure can both undercount and overcount the number of people living in poverty."

The extent of the problems of poverty and homelessness, their causes, and the best solutions are subject to much debate. Measuring the amount of poverty in the United States is an issue that has prompted divergent views. Broadly speaking, poverty is a condition in which an individual or family has a deficiency of basic necessities, such as food, water, shelter, health care, and clothing. Exactly what level of deficiency of these items constitutes a state of poverty and exactly how to measure that deficiency, however, are controversial questions for many policymakers and other experts.

In the United States, the Census Bureau sets the official federal poverty guidelines for families based on size. The family household income used to compute poverty status includes any earnings, unemployment compensation, worker's compensation, Social Security, Supplemental Security Income (SSI), public assistance, veteran's payments, survivor benefits, pension or retirement income, or other assistance. Noncash sources of income, such as food stamps and housing subsidies, however, do not count. Taking into account the size of the family and the ages of the family members, the Census Bureau determines the poverty threshold, or income level below which a household is considered to be in poverty. For example, in 2011, the poverty threshold for a single person under the age of sixty-five years old was $11,702. For a family of four that includes two children and two adults, the poverty threshold was $22,811. According to this poverty measure, 15 percent of the US population—or 46.2 million people—lived in poverty in 2011.

Many commentators believe that the poverty line set by the US Census Bureau ends up overstating the number of poor in the United States. Criticisms of the official measure include the failure to include noncash income and the focus on income rather than consumption. Rebecca M. Blank, economist and former deputy secretary in the US Department of Commerce, notes that because the poverty measure does not take into account the impact of Medicaid, food stamps, and tax deductions, it fails to provide an accurate snapshot of the extent of poverty in the country and, ironically, does not capture the effectiveness of these programs: "In the last four decades, the US has greatly expanded programs for lower-income families, including food stamps, housing vouchers, medical care assistance and tax credits. But the poverty rate doesn't take any of these resources into account because it doesn't account for taxes or noncash income."[1] Regarding the focus of the poverty measure on income, economist Nicholas Eberstadt says, "At the end of the day, poverty is about living standards, and living standards reflect consumption levels. If we really want to know about plenty and poverty in America, we should be monitoring consumption (spending patterns and the like)."[2]

On the other side, however, there are those who argue that the official US poverty measure understates the amount of poverty. Chief economist of the Service Employees International Union Mark Levinson states, "Our government's own count of the poor, while not denying their existence, also minimizes their number—not by undercounting them (though that's a factor, too) but by setting the poverty bar so low that tens of millions of poor Americans are not accounted

1. Rebecca M. Blank, "How We Measure Poverty," *Los Angeles Times*, September 15, 2008.
2. Nicholas Eberstadt, "A Poverty of Statistics," *American*, September 18, 2010. http://www.american.com/archive/2010/september/a-poverty-of-statistics.

for."[3] The National Center for Children in Poverty (NCCP) believes that the poverty threshold should be doubled: "Research consistently shows that, on average, families need an income of about twice the federal poverty level to make ends meet."[4]

Others criticize the poverty measure for both undercounting and overcounting the number of poor in the United States. Mark Greenberg of the Center for American Progress claims, "The resource-counting rules both understate and overstate resources. They fail to reflect the effects of policies such as refundable tax credits, near-cash benefits such as Supplemental Nutrition Assistance Program (formerly food stamps) or subsidized housing assistance. At the same time, they also do not consider the impact for family budgets of tax liabilities, work expenses, or health care costs."[5] In addition, Greenberg claims, "The thresholds are essentially arbitrary because they simply represent a number calculated more than 40 years ago and then adjusted for inflation, and they no longer represent anything in relation to family incomes or costs." An inaccurate poverty measure can both undercount and overcount the number of people living in poverty.

In response to some of the above concerns, the US Census Bureau and Bureau of Labor Statistics have been working together since 2009 to produce a Supplemental Poverty Measure. The Supplemental Poverty Measure will not replace the official poverty threshold rates and will not be used to determine eligibility for government programs. However, the Supplemental Poverty Measure is testing new definitions of

3. Mark Levinson, "Mismeasuring Poverty," *American Prospect*, June 25, 2012. http://prospect.org/article/mismeasuring-poverty.

4. Vanessa R. Wight, Michelle Chau, and Yumiko Aratani, "Who are America's Poor Children? The Official Story," National Center for Children in Poverty (NCCP), January 2010. http://www.nccp.org/publications/pdf/text_912.pdf.

5. Mark Greenberg, "It's Time for a Better Poverty Measure," Center for American Progress, August 25, 2009. http://www.americanprogress.org/issues/poverty/report/2009/08/25/6582/its-time-for-a-better-poverty-measure.

income thresholds and resources in order to gain a clearer picture of who is and is not living in poverty.

Similarly, defining and measuring homelessness in the United States is not a simple task. It is arguably without controversy that those who are sleeping outside, next to freeways and on downtown sidewalks, are homeless. But if a family loses their home, are they homeless when staying in the living room of a relative? And is one considered homeless after staying in a campground for several months, without a permanent home elsewhere? And once a homeless family finds shelter at a homeless shelter or within transitional housing, has the problem of homelessness been remedied? Gauging the extent of the problem of homelessness, as with measuring poverty, involves answering difficult questions about who is homeless.

Determining the correct guidelines for measuring poverty and homelessness is central in addressing these two problems. Once the poor and homeless are identified, then research into the causes of poverty and homelessness and the search for meaningful solutions can begin. By presenting different views on the extent of poverty and homelessness in the United States, the efficacy of current government programs aimed to help the poor, and other proposed solutions for combating these two problems, *Current Controversies: Poverty and Homelessness* sheds light on these ongoing social problems.

CHAPTER 1

Are Poverty and Homelessness Serious Problems?

Poverty: An Overview

Carmen DeNavas-Walt, Bernadette D. Proctor, and Jessica C. Smith

Carmen DeNavas-Walt is a statistician with the Income Statistics Branch; Bernadette D. Proctor is a statistician with the Poverty Statistics Branch; and Jessica C. Smith is a statistician with the Health and Disability Statistics Branch of the US Census Bureau.

In 2011, the official poverty rate was 15.0 percent. There were 46.2 million people in poverty.

The Change in Poverty from 2010 to 2011

After 3 consecutive years of increases, neither the official poverty rate nor the number of people in poverty were statistically different from the 2010 estimates.

The 2011 poverty rates for most demographic groups examined were not statistically different from their 2010 rates. Poverty rates were lower in 2011 than in 2010 for six groups: Hispanics, males, the foreign-born, noncitizens, people living in the South, and people living inside metropolitan statistical areas but outside principal cities. Poverty rates went up between 2010 and 2011 for naturalized citizens.

For most groups, the number of people in poverty either decreased or did not show a statistically significant change. The number of people in poverty decreased for noncitizens, people living in the South, and people living inside metropolitan statistical areas but outside principal cities between 2010 and 2011. The number of naturalized citizens in poverty increased.

Carmen DeNavas-Walt, Bernadette D. Proctor, and Jessica C. Smith, "Poverty in the United States," *Income, Poverty, and Health Insurance Coverage in the United States: 2011.* Washington, DC: US Census Bureau, US Government Printing Office, September 2012, pp. 13–19.

The poverty rate in 2011 for children under age 18 was 21.9 percent. The poverty rate for people aged 18 to 64 was 13.7 percent, while the rate for people aged 65 and older was 8.7 percent. None of the rates for these age groups were statistically different from their 2010 estimates.

Poverty Rates by Race and Hispanic Origin

The poverty rate for non-Hispanic Whites was 9.8 percent in 2011, lower than the poverty rates for other racial groups. Non-Hispanic Whites accounted for 63.2 percent of the total population but 41.5 percent of the people in poverty. For non-Hispanic Whites, neither the poverty rate nor the number of people in poverty experienced a statistically significant change between 2010 and 2011.

In 2011, 13.7 percent of people aged 18 to 64 (26.5 million) were in poverty compared with 8.7 percent of people aged 65 and older (3.6 million) and 21.9 percent of children under 18 (16.1 million).

For Blacks, the 2011 poverty rate was 27.6 percent, which represents 10.9 million people in poverty. Neither estimate was statistically different from its 2010 estimate. For Asians, the 2011 poverty rate was 12.3 percent, which represents 2.0 million people in poverty, not statistically different from the 2010 estimates. Among Hispanics, the poverty rate declined from 26.5 percent in 2010 to 25.3 percent in 2011. The number of Hispanics in poverty in 2011 was 13.2 million, not statistically different from the 2010 estimate.

Poverty Rates by Sex

In 2011, 13.6 percent of males and 16.3 percent of females were in poverty. Between 2010 and 2011, the male poverty rate decreased from 14.0 percent to 13.6 percent. The female poverty rate did not show a statistically significant change.

Gender differences in poverty rates were more pronounced for the older age group. The poverty rate for women aged 65 and older was 10.7 percent, while the poverty rate for men aged 65 and older was 6.2 percent. The poverty rate for women aged 18 to 64 was 15.5 percent, while the poverty rate for men aged 18 to 64 was 11.8 percent. For children under 18, the poverty rates for girls (22.2 percent) and boys (21.6 percent) were not statistically different from each other.

Poverty Rates by Age

In 2011, 13.7 percent of people aged 18 to 64 (26.5 million) were in poverty compared with 8.7 percent of people aged 65 and older (3.6 million) and 21.9 percent of children under 18 (16.1 million). None of these age groups experienced a statistically significant change in the number or rates of people in poverty between 2010 and 2011.

Related children are people under age 18 related to the householder by birth, marriage, or adoption who are not themselves householders or spouses of householders. The poverty rate and the number in poverty for related children under age 18 were 21.4 percent and 15.5 million in 2011, not statistically different from the 2010 estimates. For related children in families with a female householder, 47.6 percent were in poverty, compared with 10.9 percent of related children in married-couple families.

The poverty rate for those who were not U.S. citizens decreased from 26.8 percent in 2010 to 24.3 percent in 2011, and the number of noncitizens in poverty fell from 5.9 million to 5.4 million.

The poverty rate and the number in poverty for related children under age 6 were 24.5 percent and 5.8 million in 2011, not statistically different from the 2010 estimate. About 1 in 4 of these children were in poverty in 2011. More than half (57.2 percent) of related children under age 6 in families with a female householder were in poverty. This was more than four and a half times the rate of their counterparts in married-couple families (12.1 percent).

Poverty Rates by Nativity

The 2011 estimates of the poverty rate and the number in poverty for the native-born population were 14.4 percent and 38.7 million, not statistically different from the 2010 estimates. Among the foreign-born population, the poverty rate decreased from 19.9 percent in 2010 to 19.0 percent in 2011. About 7.6 million foreign-born people lived in poverty in 2011, not statistically different from the 2010 estimate.

Within the foreign-born population, 44.9 percent were naturalized U.S. citizens. For naturalized U.S. citizens, the 2011 poverty rate rose from 11.3 percent in 2010 to 12.5 percent in 2011, and the number of naturalized citizens in poverty increased from 2.0 million to 2.2 million. On the other hand, the poverty rate for those who were not U.S. citizens decreased from 26.8 percent in 2010 to 24.3 percent in 2011, and the number of noncitizens in poverty fell from 5.9 million to 5.4 million.

Poverty Rates by Region and Residence

The South was the only region to show changes in both the poverty rate and the number in poverty between 2010 and 2011. The poverty rate fell from 16.8 percent to 16.0 percent, while the number in poverty fell from 19.1 million to 18.4 million. In 2011, the poverty rates and the number in poverty for the Northeast (13.1 percent and 7.2 million), the Midwest (14.0 percent and 9.2 million), and the West (15.8 percent and 11.4 million) were not statistically different from the 2010 estimates.

Inside metropolitan statistical areas, the poverty rate and the number of people in poverty were 14.6 percent and 38.2

million in 2011, not statistically different from 2010. Among those living outside metropolitan areas, the poverty rate and the number in poverty were 17.0 percent and 8.0 million in 2011, not statistically different from 2010.

In 2011, 7.2 percent of workers aged 18 to 64 were in poverty.

Between 2010 and 2011, for those living inside metropolitan areas but not in principal cities, both the poverty rate and the number in poverty decreased from 11.9 percent and 18.9 million to 11.3 percent and 18.2 million. The 2011 poverty rate and the number of people in poverty for people in principal cities were 20.0 percent and 20.0 million, not statistically different from 2010.

Within metropolitan areas, people in poverty were more likely to live in principal cities in 2011. While 38.4 percent of all people living in metropolitan areas lived in principal cities, 52.4 percent of poor people in metropolitan areas lived in principal cities.

Poverty Rates by Work Experience and Disability Status

In 2011, 7.2 percent of workers aged 18 to 64 were in poverty. The poverty rate for those who worked full time, year round was 2.8 percent, while the poverty rate for those working less than full time, year round was 16.3 percent. None of these rates were statistically different from the 2010 poverty rates.

Among those who did not work at least 1 week last year, the poverty rate and the number in poverty were 32.9 percent and 16.1 million in 2011, not statistically different from the 2010 estimates. Those who did not work in 2011 represented 61.0 percent of people aged 18 to 64 in poverty, compared with 25.4 percent of all people aged 18 to 64.

In 2011, for people aged 18 to 64 with a disability, the poverty rate and number in poverty were 28.8 percent and 4.3 million. For people aged 18 to 64 without a disability, the poverty rate and number in poverty were 12.5 percent and 22.1 million. None of these estimates were statistically different from the 2010 estimates. Among people aged 18 to 64, those with a disability represented 16.3 percent of people in poverty, compared with 7.7 percent of all people in this age group.

The Poverty Rate of Families

In 2011, the poverty rate and the number of families in poverty were 11.8 percent and 9.5 million, both not statistically different from the 2010 estimates.

In 2011, 20.4 million people had income below one-half of their poverty threshold. They represented 6.6 percent of all people and 44.0 percent of those in poverty.

In 2011, 6.2 percent of married-couple families, 31.2 percent of families with a female householder, and 16.1 percent of families with a male householder lived in poverty. Neither the poverty rates nor the estimates of the number of families in poverty for these three family types showed any statistically significant change between 2010 and 2011.

Categorizing a person as "in poverty" or "not in poverty" is one way to describe his or her economic situation. The income-to-poverty ratio and the income deficit or surplus describe additional aspects of economic well-being. While the poverty rate shows the proportion of people with income below the appropriate poverty threshold, the income-to-poverty ratio gauges the depth of poverty and shows how close a family's income is to its poverty threshold. The income-to-poverty ratio is reported as a percentage that compares a family's or an unrelated person's income with the appropriate poverty threshold. For example, a family with an income-to-poverty ratio of 110 percent has income that is 10 percent above its poverty threshold.

The income deficit or surplus shows how many dollars a family's or an unrelated person's income is below (or above) their poverty threshold. For those with an income deficit, the measure is an estimate of the dollar amount necessary to raise a family's or a person's income to their poverty threshold. . . .

The Ratio of Income to Poverty

In 2011, 20.4 million people had income below one-half of their poverty threshold. They represented 6.6 percent of all people and 44.0 percent of those in poverty. One in 5 people (19.8 percent) had income below 125 percent of their threshold, 1 in 4 people (24.8 percent) had income below 150 percent of their poverty threshold, while approximately 1 in 3 (34.4 percent) had income below 200 percent of their threshold.

Of the 20.4 million people with income below one-half of their poverty threshold, 7.3 million were children under age 18, 12.2 million were aged 18 to 64, and 940,000 were aged 65 years and older. The percentage of people aged 65 and older with income below 50 percent of their poverty threshold was 2.3 percent, less than one-half the percentage of the total population at this poverty level (6.6 percent).

The demographic makeup of the population differs at varying degrees of poverty. In 2011, children represented 23.9 percent of the overall population; 35.6 percent of the people with income below 50 percent of their poverty threshold; 27.7 percent of the people with income between 100 percent and 200 percent of their poverty threshold; and 20.3 percent of the people with income above 200 percent of their poverty threshold. By comparison, people aged 65 and older represented 13.5 percent of the overall population; 4.6 percent of the people with income below 50 percent of their poverty threshold; 17.3 percent of the people with income between 100 percent and 200 percent of their poverty threshold; and 13.6 of the people with income above 200 percent of their poverty threshold.

The number and percentage of shared households and additional adults was higher in 2012 than in 2007, prior to the recession.

The Income Deficit for Families

The income deficit for families in poverty (the difference in dollars between a family's income and its poverty threshold) averaged $9,576 in 2011, which was not statistically different from the inflation-adjusted 2010 estimate. The average income deficit was larger for families with a female householder ($10,317) than for married-couple families ($8,887).

The average income deficit per capita for families with a female householder ($3,069) was higher than for married-couple families ($2,334). The income deficit per capita is computed by dividing the average deficit by the average number of people in that type of family. Since families with a female householder were smaller on average than married-couple families, the larger per capita deficit for female-householder families reflects their smaller average family size as well as their lower average family income.

For unrelated individuals in poverty, the average income deficit was $6,401 in 2011. The $6,169 deficit for women was lower than the $6,697 deficit for men.

The Number of Shared Households

While poverty estimates are based on income in the previous calendar year, estimates of shared households reflect household composition at the time of the survey, which is conducted during the months of February, March, and April of each year. The number and percentage of shared households and additional adults was higher in 2012 than in 2007, prior to the recession. In 2007, there were 19.7 million shared households, representing 17.0 percent of all households; by 2012, there were 22.3 million shared households, representing 18.4 percent of all households. The number of adults in shared households grew from 61.7 million (27.7 percent) in 2007 to 69.5 million (29.6 percent) in 2012.

There was no change in household sharing between 2011 and 2012. Although the total number of households increased by 1.2 million (2.5 percent), the changes in the number and percentage of total households that were shared were not statistically significant.

In 2012, an estimated 9.7 million adults aged 25 to 34 (23.6 percent) were additional adults in someone else's household. Between 2011 and 2012, the changes in the number and percentage of additional adults in this age group residing in someone else's household were not statistically significant. The number and percent of young adults in the same age group residing with their parents did not change between 2011 and 2012.

It is difficult to assess the precise impact of household sharing on overall poverty rates. In 2012, adults aged 25 to 34 living with their parents had an official poverty rate of 9.0 percent (when the entire family's income was compared with the threshold which includes the young adult as a member of the family). However, if poverty status were determined using only the additional adult's own income, 43.7 percent of those aged 25 to 34 would have been below the poverty level for a single person under age 65 ($11,702).

The poverty estimates in this report compare the official poverty thresholds to money income before taxes, not including the value of noncash benefits. The money income measure does not completely capture the economic well-being of individuals and families, and there are many questions about the adequacy of the official poverty thresholds. Families and individuals also derive economic well-being from noncash benefits, such as food and housing subsidies, and their disposable income is determined by both taxes paid and tax credits received. The official poverty thresholds developed more than 40 years ago do not take into account rising standards of living or such things as childcare expenses, other work-related expenses, variations in medical costs across population groups, or geographic differences in the cost of living. Poverty estimates using the Supplemental Poverty Measure (SPM) address many of these concerns.

Poverty in America
Is Unacceptably High

Bernie Sanders

Bernie Sanders has served as US Senator from Vermont since 2007.

The crisis of poverty in America is one of the great moral and economic issues facing our country. It is very rarely talked about in the mainstream media. It gets even less attention in Congress. Why should people care? Many poor people don't vote. They certainly don't make large campaign contributions, and they don't have powerful lobbyists representing their interests.

Poverty in America

Here's why we all should care. There are 46 million Americans—about one in six—living below the poverty line. That's the largest number on record, according to a new report released Tuesday [September 13, 2011] by the Census Bureau. About 49.9 million Americans lacked health insurance, the report also said. That number has soared by 13.3 million since 2000.

Moreover, according to the Organization for Economic Cooperation and Development [OECD], the United States has both the highest overall poverty rate and the highest childhood poverty rate of any major industrialized country on earth. This comes at a time when the U.S. also has the most unequal distribution of wealth and income of any major country on earth with the top 1 percent earning more than the bottom 50 percent.

Bernie Sanders, "Is Poverty a Death Sentence?," *Common Dreams*, September 14, 2011. commondreams.org. Reproduced by permission.

According to the latest figures [2009] from the OECD, 21.6 percent of American children live in poverty. This compares to 3.7 percent in Denmark, 5 percent in Finland, 5.5 percent in Norway 6.9 percent in Slovenia, 7 percent in Sweden, 7.2 percent [in] Hungary, 8.3 percent in Germany, 8.8 percent in the Czech Republic, 9.3 percent in France, 9.4 percent in Switzerland. I suppose we can take some comfort in that our numbers are not quite as bad as Turkey (23.5 percent), Chile (24 percent) and Mexico (25.8 percent).

Poverty in America today is a death sentence for tens and tens of thousands of our people.

When we talk about poverty in America, we think about people who may be living in substandard and overcrowded homes or may be homeless. We think about people who live with food insecurity, who may not know how they are going to feed themselves or their kids tomorrow. We think about people who, in cold states like Vermont, may not have enough money to purchase the fuel they need to keep warm in the winter. We think about people who cannot afford health insurance or access to medical care. We think about people who cannot afford an automobile or transportation, and can't get to their job or the grocery store. We think about senior citizens who may have to make a choice between buying the prescription drugs he or she needs, or purchasing an adequate supply of food.

Poverty as a Death Sentence

I want to focus on an enormously important point. And that is that poverty in America today leads not only to anxiety, unhappiness, discomfort and a lack of material goods. It leads to death. Poverty in America today is a death sentence for tens and tens of thousands of our people which is why the high childhood poverty rate in our country is such an outrage.

Some facts:

- At a time when we are seeing major medical breakthroughs in cancer and other terrible diseases for the people who can afford those treatments, the reality is that life expectancy for low-income women has declined over the past 20 years in 313 counties in our country. In other words, in some areas of America, women are now dying at a younger age than they used to.

- In America today, people in the highest income group level, the top 20 percent, live, on average, at least 6.5 years longer than those in the lowest income group. Let me repeat that. If you are poor in America you will live 6.5 years less than if you are wealthy or upper-middle class.

- In America today, adult men and women who have graduated from college can expect to live at least 5 years longer than people who have not finished high school.

- In America today, tens of thousands of our fellow citizens die unnecessarily because they cannot get the medical care they need. According to Reuters, "nearly 45,000 people die in the United States each year—one every 12 minutes—in large part because they lack health insurance and cannot get good care. Harvard Medical School researchers found in an analysis released on Thursday [September 17, 2009]."

- In 2009, the infant mortality rate for African American infants was twice that of white infants.

I recite these facts because I believe that as bad as the current situation is with regard to poverty, it will likely get worse in the immediate future. As a result of the greed, recklessness and illegal behavior of Wall Street we are now in the midst of the worst economic downturn since the 1930s. Millions of workers have lost their jobs and have slipped out of the middle class and into poverty. Poverty is increasing.

From a moral perspective, it is not acceptable that we allow so much unnecessary suffering and preventable death to continue.

The Existing Safety Net

Further, despite the reality that our deficit problem has been caused by the recession and declining revenue, two unpaid for wars and tax breaks for the wealthy, there are some in Congress who wish to decimate the existing safety net which provides a modicum of security for the elderly, the sick, the children and lower income people. Despite an increase in poverty, some of these people would like to cut or end Social Security, Medicare, Medicaid, food stamps, home heating assistance, nutrition programs and help for the disabled and the homeless.

To the degree that they are successful, there is no question in my mind that many more thousands of men, women and children will die.

From a moral perspective, it is not acceptable that we allow so much unnecessary suffering and preventable death to continue. From an economic perspective and as we try to fight our way out of this terrible recession, it makes no sense that we push to the fringe so many people who could be of such great help to us.

Poverty Is Increasing Among Young Families with Children

Andrew M. Sum

Andrew M. Sum is professor of economics and director of the Center for Labor Market Studies at Northeastern University in Boston.

Earlier this month [September 2011], the U.S. Census Bureau released its findings on the annual incomes, earnings, and poverty status of the nation's population in 2010. On the poverty front, the news was not good. For the third straight year in a row, the number of people of all ages living in poverty rose, reaching 46.2 million individuals in 2010, a record high number, equivalent to 15.1 percent of the national population.

Poverty Among Young Families with Children

While poverty problems have risen since the onset of the Great Recession in late 2007 for nearly every major age, gender, and race-ethnic group, the increases in poverty have been most severe among the nation's youngest families (those headed by an adult under 30 years old) especially those with one or more own children present in the home. Between 2007 and 2010, the overall poverty rate for U.S. families rose from 9.8 percent to 11.7 percent, a gain of nearly two full percentage points. These increases in family poverty rates varied quite widely across different age groups of families and by the presence of children. Among the nation's older families (head 65

Andrew M. Sum, "The Impact of Rising Poverty on the Nation's Young Families and Their Children, 2000–2010," *Children's Defense Fund Policy Brief #1*, September 2011.

35

or older), the poverty rate was unchanged between 2007 and 2010 at 5.7 percent. Among families headed by a person 30–64 years old with no children present, the poverty rate rose by only 1.3 percentage points to 6.7 percent. Among all young families with a head under 30 years of age, the poverty rate rose by a considerably higher 6 percentage points and among young families with one or more children in the home it rose by nearly 8 percentage points to 37.3 percent in 2010.

By the end of the decade, family poverty rates in the U.S. varied widely across families based on the age of the family head and the presence of children. These family poverty rates ranged from a low of 5.7 percent among the nation's older families to a high of 37.3 percent among young families with children, a relative difference of 6.5 times from top to bottom.

By 2010, slightly more than one-third of the nation's young families were poor or near poor.

Poverty Rates in Recent Decades

The deterioration in poverty rates among U.S. families was quite severe over the entire past decade. After making great strides in reducing poverty during the national economic boom from 1993–2000, including among the young, the incidence of poverty was sharply higher among families in 2010 than in 2000. All major family groups faced a higher poverty rate in 2010 than they did in 2000 near the peak of the economic cycle. However, again the size of these poverty rate increases varied widely across age and presence of children [groups of families]. Among older families, the poverty rate rose by only .4 percentage points, among families with a head 30–64 years old with no children present in the home it rose by only 1.7 percentage points, but if at least one child was present in the home of such families the poverty rate jumped by 4.4 percentage points or nearly 45 percent. Among the nation's youngest families with children, the incidence of poverty jumped by close to 12 percentage points to 37.3 percent, *the highest poverty rate ever recorded for this age group dating back to 1967 when it stood at only 14 percent.*

Over the past four decades, the age structure of poverty rates in the U.S. has changed dramatically with the elderly typically facing lower poverty rates and the nation's children becoming more deeply mired in poverty. In his late 1980s book *Family and Nation*, the late U.S. Senator Patrick Moynihan remarked that "It is fair to assume that the U.S. has become the first society in history where a person is more likely to be poor if young than old". Comparing the poverty rates of young families with children with those of the nation's older families from 1967 to 2010 clearly confirms Moynihan's argument. In 1967, only 14 percent of the nation's young families with children were poor versus approximately 11 percent of the nation's older families, a ratio of about 1.3–1. By 1979, this relative family poverty ratio had risen to nearly 2.4 to 1, it would increase further to 4.4 to 1 by 1989; to 4.8 to 1 in 2000 and to 6.5 to 1 in 2010 the highest such ratio in the past 44 years for which such official poverty data are available.

The Effects of Income Inadequacy

The income inadequacy problems of the nation's young families are not confined simply to those of the poor. The past decade has also witnessed sharp increases in poverty/near poverty and low income problems among the nation's young families, especially those with children. By 2010, slightly more than one-third of the nation's young families were poor or near poor, up by nearly 10 percentage points from the beginning of the decade and a slight majority (51 percent) had low annual incomes; i.e., below 200 percent of the poverty line. *Among young families with children residing in the home, 4 of every 9 were poor or near poor and close to 2 out of 3 were low income in 2010.*

The High fraction of American children living in young families with severe income inadequacy problems will have long-lasting negative effects on the children's cognitive achievement, the children's educational attainment, the children's nutrition, physical and mental health, and social behavior. For example, test score gaps between children in affluent and low-income families have been widening over the years and the incomes and wealth of families have become increasingly important determinants of adolescents' high school graduation, college attendance, and college persistence and graduation. The share of adolescents from poor families and with bottom quartile academic skills obtaining bachelor degrees by their mid-20s has come close to zero. These are grave outcomes with serious long-term consequences for America's economic and social future.

There Is a Housing Affordability Crisis in America

Patrick Markee

Patrick Markee is a senior policy analyst at the Coalition for the Homeless in New York City and a member of the board of directors of the National Coalition for the Homeless.

For an up-close view of the affordable housing crisis—which predated the mortgage-driven financial crisis of 2008 but has deepened since then into a full-blown national emergency—one place to be was the Jesse Owens Memorial Complex in the Red Bird neighborhood of Dallas [Texas]. There, in the early morning hours of a typically scorching day this past July [2011], thousands of impoverished Texans lined up for a chance to get on a waiting list for federal housing assistance, the first time in five years that the county government had accepted applications. Back in May another 21,000 people had applied for a shot at 5,000 spots on the Dallas Housing Authority's waiting list—still better odds than in nearby Plano, where 8,000 people applied for only 100 available housing vouchers.

Evidence of a Housing Crisis

Similar gatherings, with similar casinolike odds, have occurred around the country with a sort of stealthy frequency. In Oakland, California, which opened its waiting list in January, officials expected as many as 100,000 people to apply for 10,000 vouchers. In Atlanta [Georgia], sixty-two people were injured in 2010 at an East Point shopping center where 30,000 lined up after the local housing authority opened its waiting list for the first time in eight years. Even small communities like

Patrick Markee, "The Unfathomable Cuts in Housing Aid," *The Nation*, January 2, 2012.

Aiken, South Carolina, saw hundreds queuing up in October for a chance at housing aid about as likely as seeing three cherries in a row on a Vegas slot machine.

In the midst of rising homelessness, rampant joblessness and the lingering foreclosure crisis, Congress recently slashed the federal housing agency's budget by $3.8 billion.

Another way you can find tangible evidence of the housing affordability crunch is by visiting one of New York City's exploding number of homeless shelters, where a record 41,000 homeless people bed down each night, including more than 17,000 children. The *New York Times* recently told the story of one of those children, fourth-grader N-Dia Layne, who travels two and a half hours each day between her Upper Manhattan shelter and her school in Brooklyn's Brownsville neighborhood. In Cleveland [Ohio], the number of homeless families and kids grew so rapidly this past summer that for the first time shelters were forced to eliminate daytime meals, housing-search assistance and other services in order to move workers to the overnight shifts, according to Brian Davis of the Northeast Ohio Coalition for the Homeless.

You'll find another, even less-noticed symptom of the housing crisis scattered in the rising number of foreclosed homes that have been "occupied"—in defiance of banks and legal authorities—by former owners and other displaced people. From Rochester, New York, to Minneapolis [Minnesota] to Miami [Florida] and back to Oakland, more and more people have come to the logical conclusion that one solution to the housing crisis is to settle down in vacant homes seized by banks. Some of these occupations, like those organized by groups like Take Back the Land, are part of an organized resistance to banks and mortgage lenders. Community groups recently joined with Occupy Wall Street protesters to help a homeless family in Brooklyn's East New York neighbor-hood move into a foreclosed home that has sat vacant for three years. Some other "occupations"—as in the case of a woman in Fort Bend County, Texas, facing criminal charges—involve people at the end of their rope merely trying to keep a roof over their head. Indeed, in Las Vegas [Nevada], which has one of the highest foreclosure rates in the country, some 300 families are evicted each day by the constable's office, many of them people who have been hanging on to seized homes.

Goverment Response to the Housing Crisis

The one place you won't hear any discussion, much less ac-knowledgment, of the nation's spiraling housing affordability crisis is around Washington, DC, by its political class and its media enablers. There the conference rooms and cable news studios echo with talk of deficit reduction via sharp budget cuts, with special relish for so-called discretionary programs like housing assistance. Indeed, in the midst of rising home-lessness, rampant joblessness and the lingering foreclosure cri-sis, Congress recently slashed the federal housing agency's budget by $3.8 billion.

"For the past decade federal housing programs have been treading water," says Doug Rice, a housing policy expert at the Center for Budget and Policy Priorities, "while need among low-income families has grown at an alarming rate." Indeed, the nation's housing affordability crunch was severe even be-fore the "lesser depression" struck. Now, amid rising poverty and the anemic recovery-in-name-only, housing-starved Americans face another threat: deeper cutbacks to federal housing assistance as part of the bipartisan obsession with budget deficits. "Today the housing safety net isn't just frayed," says Neil Donovan, executive director of the National Coali-tion for the Homeless. "It's missing. And still everyone's being told to walk the tightrope without any net."

By nearly any measure, there are fewer and fewer homes affordable to working-class and poor Americans. The federal housing agency's annual assessment finds that "worst-case housing needs" grew by 42 percent from 2001 to 2009, and nationwide there is a shortfall of nearly 3.5 million housing units for the poorest households. According to Harvard University's Joint Center for Housing Studies, the share of renter households with the most severe cost burdens—that is, where more than half of income goes to rent and utilities— grew from a fifth to a quarter over the past decade and has doubled in the past half-century. And as household incomes stagnated for most of the past decade and then dropped during the economic crisis, the nation saw its already inadequate stock of cheap rental housing shrink even faster.

The Federal Housing Budget

Confronting this yawning affordability gap, the government did almost nothing. Congress managed to beat back some of the [George W.] Bush administration's more egregious proposals, like converting housing programs into block grants. But a decade later, federal housing aid reaches barely the same number of households, despite population growth and worsening need. This form of malign neglect has also led to the deterioration of much of the nation's vital public housing stock, where the unpaid maintenance and repair bill tops $26 billion and translates into leaky roofs, failing boilers, broken windows and the loss of thousands of apartments. In Cleveland, says Davis of the Northeast Ohio Coalition, the repair backlog means that public housing units sit vacant, leaving hundreds of families stranded each year on a waiting list that's already 11,000 households strong.

In the wake of this lost decade, Congress's recent cut of $3.8 billion from the housing budget is the fiscal equivalent of a gut punch. According to the Center for Budget and Policy Priorities, the cutback represents a remarkable 9.2 percent reduction in a budget that is "lower than any [federal housing] budget since 2003, in inflation-adjusted terms." The programs that took the biggest hits are public housing repair and maintenance, production of affordable homes, and housing assistance for seniors and people with disabilities. And although the largest federal rental assistance program, Housing Choice Vouchers, avoided the most draconian cuts, there's no doubt that voucher waiting lists will continue to grow nationwide.

Among affordable housing advocates, optimism about the coming years is in short supply; the mood is nearer to resigned desperation.

The punishing housing budget for 2012 offers a taste of what is to come as a result of the Congressional Republicans' success holding the country hostage during this past summer's debt ceiling standoff. The deal struck to raise the debt ceiling, and the pre-Thanksgiving collapse of the "supercommittee," triggers nine years of cuts to discretionary programs like housing aid. Indeed, according to OMB Watch [now Center for Effective Government], beginning in 2013 the budget deal will cut discretionary programs by 14 percent and may lead to a nearly $6 billion reduction for housing programs.

Although housing assistance takes only one penny of every federal budget dollar, right-wing ideologues since at least the [President Ronald] Reagan years have long used "deficit reduction" as a pretext for achieving their dream of eliminating government housing aid. Reagan infamously slashed the housing budget at a time of recession and the emergence of modern homelessness, while the deficit exploded. There's no question that when it comes to housing assistance, the Reagan legacy lives on. This year the Cato Institute outlined a plan to tackle the budget deficit that would, among other things, "terminate" the Department of Housing and Urban Development.

And Reagan's Tea Party descendants in Congress promise further chops of the budget ax for housing and other safety net programs.

The Focus of Homeless Advocates

Among affordable housing advocates, optimism about the coming years is in short supply; the mood is nearer to resigned desperation. As Sheila Crowley, longtime president of the National Low Income Housing Coalition, recently wrote to her members, "I can say with certainty that there has been no time in my memory when the core federal programs that help poor people keep body and soul together have been under such threat." Even the advocates' major victory of recent years—legislation passed in 2008 to create a National Housing Trust Fund aimed at building millions of affordable homes—is still caught in the twin snares of deficit hysteria and the fallout from the foreclosure crisis. Congress has not authorized start-up funding, something unlikely to happen in the current austerity environment, while long-term financing of the trust fund remains uncertain. In the near term, advocates are mostly fighting rear-guard actions, hoping to forestall the most devastating cutbacks and trying to work around Tea Party zealots in Congress.

> *Sadly, many Obama administration officials have adopted the subpopulations approach, switching the focus of federal homeless policy to military veterans.*

More controversially, many Beltway [Washington, DC, area] homeless advocates and trade associations over much of the past decade have largely abandoned efforts to address the fundamental causes of homelessness. Instead of broad campaigns to tackle the housing affordability crisis, these groups and some large foundations have focused on smaller efforts targeting homeless subpopulations. This narrow approach was championed by the Bush administration's charismatic and divisive "homelessness czar," Phil Mangano, who prioritized programs aimed at the "chronically homeless"—mainly mentally ill long-term street dwellers. Mangano and his trade-group allies hectored states and localities to develop "ten-year plans" to end homelessness but did next to nothing to back up the plans with housing resources. Indeed, Mangano preached the ten-year-plan gospel as the Bush administration was taking the knife to federal housing programs.

Nearly a decade later, there's mounting evidence of the failures of the underfunded ten-year plans, most starkly in the soaring number of homeless children, families and working poor who were largely left out of Mangano's approach. And an emerging chorus of local and national homeless advocates are criticizing the narrow Beltway focus on subpopulations. Donovan of the National Coalition for the Homeless calls it a "cowardly way of not admitting that we're not devoting the resources we need to do the job" and says it's an "abusive way of doing social policy" that fails to address the scope and causes of the homeless crisis.

Sadly, many [Barack] Obama administration officials have adopted the subpopulations approach, switching the focus of federal homeless policy to military veterans. The 100,000 Homes Campaign, launched in 2010 with corporate and foundation backing, is emblematic of the lingering PR [public relations] appeal as well as the fundamental limits of the subpopulations approach. The campaign has been the subject of fawning mainstream press reports, even though its goal of finding 100,000 homes over three years would address the needs of only a small fraction of the estimated 3.5 million Americans who are homeless every year.

The National Discourse About Income Inequality

Despite the bleak policy landscape and the worsening affordability crisis, many local advocates and people working on the front lines talk about the renewed energy and hope generated by the nascent Occupy movement and the revived national discourse about income inequality. Donovan talks hopefully about the "other 1 percent"—the homeless and poor—saying that the concentration of wealth and power in the hands of the superrich 1 percent is "causing the other 1 percent to agitate, and to show that homeless people are something other than a herded mass. They're saying, Enough is enough."

It may be only a flicker of hope, but it appeared to resonate in the first Occupy encampments, from Zuccotti Park to Oakland to the nation's capital, where poor and homeless people were a significant presence. Donovan tells the story of one Occupy DC participant, who spoke out at an October protest: "This homeless US marine stands up and says, I fought for the entire country. And in the service I was taught not to leave anyone behind. So I say, Don't house only homeless veterans—house everyone!"

Poverty Has Declined Over the Last Few Decades

Bruce D. Meyer and James X. Sullivan

Bruce D. Meyer is the McCormick Professor of Public Policy at the University of Chicago's Harris School of Public Policy Studies and James X. Sullivan is an associate professor in the economics department at the University of Notre Dame.

Over the past three decades, the American economy has grown considerably. Accounting for population growth and price changes, GDP [gross domestic product] has increased by more than 60 percent. There is a prevailing sentiment, however, that the middle class and the poor have not enjoyed any of the benefits of this sustained growth. A 2007 CBS News poll found that 60 percent of Americans believed that things had gotten worse for the middle class during the past decade. With the financial collapse of 2008 and the recession that followed it, that percentage is surely much higher today. Conventional wisdom holds that things have also gotten worse for those at the bottom, despite efforts to alleviate the living conditions of the poor. As Robert Siegel, of National Public Radio, recently stated, "It is commonplace to say that we have lost the war on poverty."

The Official Measures of Poverty

Much of this sentiment stems from official measures that paint a bleak picture of the middle class and the poor. Official median household income fell between 1999 and 2004, using the conventional adjustment for inflation. Since then, median income has risen but remains below its 1999 level. Official sta-

Bruce D. Meyer and James X. Sullivan, "American Mobility: An Untold Story of Progress for America's Middle Class and Poor," *Commentary*, vol. 133, no. 3, March 2012, pp. 30–34. Reproduced by permission.

tistics are even gloomier for the poor: The official poverty rate in 2009 was higher than in 1980.

But this grim portrait of an America in which life has improved for the wealthy and no one else is inaccurate. Over the past three decades, growth in the U.S. economy has produced considerable, and demonstrable, improvement in material well-being for both the middle class and the poor. They, too, have come along for the ride. One just needs to know where—and how—to look.

With analytical measures that are great advancements on the official methods of the past, we have found in our research significant evidence of such improvement among the middle class and poor. Between 1980 and 2009, income and consumption rose by more than 50 percent in real terms for both groups. Living units became markedly larger and much more likely to feature air-conditioning and other amenities. The quality of the cars these families own also improved considerably.

The Material Well-Being of Americans

First, we've found strong evidence of improvement in the material well-being of poor families. For Americans in the 10th percentile of wealth, income rose by 44 percent between 1980 and 2009. Even this, however, understates improvements at the bottom. Consumption among the poorest (what goods they actually obtained or used) grew even more during this same period. For those in the bottom 20 percent, or the lowest quintile, the size of living units increased by 200 to 250 square feet, and the fraction of these low-income people who enjoy either central or window air-conditioning doubled. The share with other amenities also rose noticeably.

There were similar improvements for the middle class. Their houses have become bigger, rising by more than one-quarter of a room without adjusting for household size, and by seven-tenths of a room when accounting for family size.

Since 1989, square footage has risen between 300 and 350 square feet. About half of this increase has taken place since 1999, a period during which official median household income fell.

> *Most analyses of economic well-being rely on narrow income measures that do not reflect the full range of resources ... available to the households for consumption of goods and services.*

The share of middle-quintile individuals with air-conditioning rose from 58 percent to 88 percent between 1981 and 2009. Central air-conditioning rose from 27 percent to 67 percent. Since 1989, the share of people in the middle quintile with a dishwasher has risen from 53 percent to 70 percent; and with a clothes dryer from 79 percent to 88 percent. Again, a large share of this increase has occurred since 1999. Since 1989, the incidence of leaks from plumbing and roofs has fallen sharply, as has the likelihood of living amid peeling paint or with a broken toilet.

The Problem with Official Analyses

What accounts for the striking differences between official analyses and our research? First, most analyses of economic well-being rely on narrow income measures that do not reflect the full range of resources, monetary and otherwise, available to the households for consumption of goods and services.

They ignore food stamps and do not take into account resources from important antipoverty programs such as the Earned Income Tax Credit (EITC) and housing or school-lunch subsidies. These excluded benefits are generous and have increased significantly over the past few decades. Official analyses also often rely on underreported measures of income. For these reasons, our analyses include comparisons between official pretax income numbers and figures that incorporate taxes and benefits.

Second, official statistics exaggerate inflation. Obviously, the higher prices seem, the lower the perceived purchasing power of the poor. But in determining the poverty threshold—the statistical point that separates the poor from the rest of the population—the official statistics rely on an index called the Consumer Price Index for All Urban Consumers, also known as CPI-U. There is broad consensus that the CPI-U overstates inflation and therefore significantly understates improvements in economic well-being. When median incomes are calculated, a similarly biased index is used: the Consumer Price Index Research Series, or CPI-U-RS. Over time, bias in both these indices has significantly muted the rise in household income for both the middle class and the poor.

We believe that consumption provides a more appropriate measure of well-being than does income.

Hypothetically, an annual misstating of inflation by just 1 percent would lead to a 33 percent difference in determining median incomes between 1980 and 2009. Our best evidence indicates that the annual bias over much of this period has been even greater. In 1996, the Boskin Commission, a group of eminent economists appointed by the Senate Finance Committee, concluded that the annual bias in the CPI-U was 1.1 percentage points that year, but 1.3 percentage points in preceding years. In our results, we make changes to correct for such bias by using an adjustment that subtracts 0.8 percentage points from the growth as figured in the CPI-U-RS index each year.

The Importance of Consumption Data

Finally, we believe that consumption provides a more appropriate measure of well-being than does income. It reflects resources that may have been accumulated over time, whereas income may vary in the short term. Consider, for example, a retired couple who own their home outright and who live off of savings. Clearly, their *income* will not reflect the totality of their actual *material well-being.*

Income measures also fail to capture disparities in consumption that result from differences in the amount of credit available and credit used. Even if income remains the same, government safety-net programs affect the ability of households to consume because they diminish the need for households to save for a rainy day. (If you know you're going to receive free health care from the time you're 65, you do not have to restrict your spending in the prior two decades to save for health-care expenses, for example.) Consumption is more likely to capture income from self-employment and to reflect private and government transfers. Much of the effort to improve income measures involves making them more like consumption measures, but it is much easier to begin with consumption data. That's what we did.

Our preferred measures of income and consumption as well as data on housing and cars all tell the same story: The material circumstances of the middle class have improved dramatically since 1980. It is crucial to note the pattern of differences between the results from official reports and those from our improved measures. We've therefore provided three different assessments for comparison.

First, official pretax median household income grew by 20 percent in real terms between 1980 and 2000, but then fell by 5 percent during the 2000s. The second measure of pretax money income differs from the first in several ways: Resources are measured at the *family*, rather than household, level and adjusted for differences in family size and composition following National Academy of Sciences recommendations. The median for this second measure follows a pattern very similar to that of the official measure, although the level of the median is about 15 percent higher.

The third measure, unlike the first two, accounts for inflation using our adjusted inflation index rather than the biased CPI-U-RS. When the adjusted index is used, median income is seen to have risen by 46 percent between 1980 and 2009, compared with 17 percent when the biased measure is used.

All our results indicate a notable rise in the material well-being of the poor during the past three decades.

It's not the rich 1 percent who have been working to stall the well-being of the middle class; it's bad statistics.

A Rise in Material Well-Being

In terms of car ownership—the largest and most expensive consumer product—those in the middle-income quintile, or the middle 20 percent, have fared well. Car ownership rates for this quintile are high—close to 95 percent—and have not changed noticeably during the past three decades. But the fraction of families with more than one car rose by more than 4.4 percentage points between 1999 and 2009. Furthermore, these cars were much more likely to have features such as power brakes, power steering, and a sunroof. The number of cars with air-conditioning rose from 47 percent to more than 83 percent between 1981 and 2004. These changes in vehicle characteristics understate the full pattern of quality improvement. There have been widespread improvements in braking and acceleration, as well as in the adoption of air bags, antilock brakes, sophisticated sound systems, and other features. Any discussion of material well-being must take into account these advances in amenities. If the material comforts of high earners can be cited as the excesses of a carefree elite, then honesty demands consideration of the dramatically improved products that are increasingly available to Americans across the economic spectrum.

All our results indicate a notable rise in the material well-being of the poor during the past three decades. Using our preferred measures of income and consumption (and addressing bias in previous methods of calculating inflation), we've shown a sharp decline in poverty. We've also shown that there have been noticeable improvements in the quality of living units and cars for poor families.

The official measure of pretax money income for America's poorest 10 percent indicates only modest gains over the past three decades. We see virtually no change between 1980 and 1993. The 10th percentile for the official measure then rose by 19 percent between 1993 and 1999, but it fell in real terms in the most recent decade. But, after making the same adjustments made to the middle-class results, we can see that the income of the 10th percentile has actually risen by 40 percent.

A Decline in Poverty

The consumption numbers indicate significantly improved well-being for those near the bottom over most of our time period. Between 1980 and 2009, consumption among the 10th percentile rose by 54 percent in real terms, while after-tax income plus noncash benefits grew by 44 percent. The changes in consumption have often differed from the changes in income, particularly in recent years. During the 2000s, consumption at the 10th percentile grew by 18 percent, while after-tax income plus noncash benefits grew by less than 4 percent.

Taxes and transfer payments (such as the Earned Income Tax Credit) have had an important impact on the resources of those near the bottom. The 10th percentile of after-tax income plus noncash benefits rose noticeably more than did the 10th percentile of pretax income, and the results showing after-tax income and noncash benefits show a consistently higher level of material well-being for those at the bottom.

Elsewhere, we show that this difference is accounted for by taxes rather than noncash benefits.

When we looked at poverty rates, we found striking results. According to the official measures, the poverty rate in the United States between 1980 and 2009 increased by more than 1 percentage point. By our calculations using our adjusted inflation measure, poverty levels fell by more than 3 percentage points. And, even more striking, over the past three decades, a measure of what we might call "consumption poverty"—or the fraction of individuals whose consumption falls below an inflation-adjusted poverty threshold—fell by nearly 10 percentage points, a decline of 76 percent.

An Improvement in Living Standards

Like their middle-class counterparts, those in the bottom income quintile are living—and driving—much better than they were 30 years ago. Their houses have become bigger, rising by 0.16 rooms on average without adjusting for household size, and by half a room when accounting for family size. Housing-unit size rose after 1999, but by a smaller amount than over the previous decade.

> *The national crisis as it is currently framed—as one of declining well-being for the middle class and the poor—is not supported by rigorous analysis.*

The share of bottom-quintile individuals with any air-conditioning rose from 41 percent to 83 percent between 1981 and 2009. Central air-conditioning rose by 39 percentage points from 15 percent to 54 percent. Since 1989, the share of people in the bottom quintile with a dishwasher rose from 22 percent to 42 percent, and the prevalence of clothes dryers for the bottom quintile rose from 48 percent to 68 percent. Most of this increase occurred after 1999, a period during which official poverty *rose*. Over the period since 1989, the incidence of plumbing and roofing leaks fell sharply, as did the likelihood of living amid peeling paint or with a broken-down toilet.

Over the past three decades, car-ownership rates grew more noticeably among the poor than among the middle class. In 1981, 69 percent of all households in the bottom quintile owned at least one car. By 2009, 76 percent did. There is also evidence that the quality of cars owned has improved. Among the poorest households, the fraction of cars with power brakes, power steering, or other features rose sharply between 1981 and 2004. The fraction of cars with air-conditioning rose from 47 percent to 77 percent between 1980 and 2004. The share of cars with power brakes, power steering, and air-conditioning was about the same for the bottom and middle quintiles by 2004.

These patterns stand in sharp contrast to the noticeable decline in living standards over the past few years, which have hurt both the poor and middle class. Since 2007, median consumption has fallen by 5 percent, and consumption poverty has increased by 21 percent. Many of the calls for radical policy reform have been based on these short-term patterns. But the national crisis as it is currently framed—as one of declining well-being for the middle class and the poor—is not supported by rigorous analysis.

If discussion of wealth inequality is to bear fruit and lead to effective policy, it must begin with this honest assessment and not the politicized impressions that have made genuine debate impossible. The recent declines in the material circumstances of the middle class and the poor are due to a severe recession and a sluggish recovery. These short-term setbacks, while very real, do not offset the long-run picture of American progress that is broad and dramatic.

Poverty Is Not as High as the Government Claims It Is

Bloomberg View

Bloomberg View is part of the Bloomberg news service, which provides information to newspapers and magazines worldwide.

Poverty statistics can be used to prove almost anything.

When the U.S. Census Bureau reported last week [September 12, 2012] that 46 million Americans, or 15 percent of the population, live in poverty, conservatives said that five decades of the welfare state have had virtually no effect. Liberals answered that laissez-faire economics have kept poverty rates stubbornly high.

This debate is based on a false premise: Poverty isn't as high as the U.S. government says it is. The reason is that federal programs, supported by Democrats and Republicans alike, have dramatically reduced poverty and, by extension, income inequality.

To understand why, let's look at what the numbers don't show. The Census Bureau doesn't count safety-net benefits, including food stamps, housing aid, school lunches and other noncash transfers. Adding the cash value of food stamps alone would lower the poverty population by 3.9 million people. Census data also overcompensate for inflation by ignoring discount prices at big-box outlets such as Wal-Mart Stores Inc., where many low-income families shop. The figures don't even factor in Medicare and Medicaid benefits.

Most Overlooked

But tax credits are the most overlooked numbers of all. One, the Earned Income Tax Credit, is refundable, meaning that some low-income breadwinners get a check from the Internal Revenue Service even if their earnings are so small that they owe no income tax. Counting that tax credit would decrease the number of people living in poverty by another 5.7 million.

The Census Bureau defines a family of four with income less than $23,021 as impoverished. But a better portrait of poverty in America would count all government benefits and tax credits, raising many households' income considerably. An even truer picture of deprivation would measure consumption (how much a household spends on rent, autos, food and other items) rather than income (how much a household admits to bringing home in earnings). Incomes are unreliable because people are reluctant to reveal how much they make. They are less reticent when asked if they have television sets, cars and air conditioning, or if they eat out and go to movies.

If poverty figures are overstated, . . . then so is income inequality.

When adjusted for these flaws, the level of poverty is much lower, says a new paper by economists Bruce D. Meyer at the University of Chicago and James X. Sullivan at the University of Notre Dame. Instead of 15 percent, it is only 4 percent to 5 percent. And instead of being higher than it was in 1980, poverty has declined by two-thirds.

In other words, the war on poverty hasn't been won, but it's making inroads. The lion's share of the credit, the professors conclude, goes to the Earned Income Tax Credit, the Child Tax Credit and Social Security.

This may not jibe with Republican presidential nominee Mitt Romney's quip about the "culture of dependency," a trait he ascribed to a remarkable 47 percent of voters. The opposite is true: Anti-poverty programs have reduced dependency and encouraged work—and can be fashioned to work even better.

One option is to strengthen the Earned Income Tax Credit. It began under one Republican president (Gerald Ford), was improved by another (Ronald Reagan), and was made refundable by a Democrat (Bill Clinton)—in each case with the support of congressional Republicans. Studies show the tax credit was the most important factor in reducing welfare rolls, even more so than the 1996 welfare-reform law. Now geared toward single-parent families, the credit could be expanded to help two-parent families and parents without custody of their children.

Important Stabilizers

Automatic stabilizers are also important and shouldn't be undermined, as the budget blueprint by U.S. Representative Paul Ryan, Romney's running mate, would do. As *Bloomberg View* columnist Peter Orszag has written, eligibility for food stamps, unemployment insurance and relief to state governments should expand automatically, without waiting for Congress to act, when the economy is weak.

The implications of all this go beyond politics. Poverty statistics are one of the U.S.'s most closely watched indicators of economic well-being. They can help tell us if poverty-fighting programs are working, or if our taxes are being wasted. They can also steer policy-setters toward more productive solutions and away from popular yet misguided ideas.

If poverty figures are overstated, for example, then so is income inequality. The most-cited studies don't count government benefits or employer-provided health insurance. There is little doubt that the chasm between the top 1 percent and the 99 percenters is narrower than we have been led to believe. That shouldn't depress liberals or cheer conservatives: The inequality gap is closing because of government programs, not the stagnant incomes of the private sector.

Poverty and Homelessness Are Not Serious Problems in America

Robert Rector and Rachel Sheffield

Robert Rector is a senior research fellow and Rachel Sheffield is a research associate at the Heritage Foundation.

Today [September 13, 2011], the Census Bureau released its annual poverty report, which declared that a record 46.2 million (roughly one in seven) Americans were poor in 2010. The numbers were up sharply from the previous year's total of 43.6 million. Although the current recession has greatly increased the numbers of the poor, high levels of poverty predate the recession. In most years for the past two decades, the Census Bureau has declared that at least 35 million Americans lived in poverty.

The Living Conditions of the Poor

However, understanding poverty in America requires looking behind these numbers at the actual living conditions of the individuals the government deems to be poor. For most Americans, the word "poverty" suggests near destitution: an inability to provide nutritious food, clothing, and reasonable shelter for one's family. But only a small number of the 46 million persons classified as "poor" by the Census Bureau fit that description. While real material hardship certainly does occur, it is limited in scope and severity.

The following are facts about persons defined as "poor" by the Census Bureau as taken from various government reports:

- 80 percent of poor households have air conditioning. In

1970, only 36 percent of the entire U.S. population enjoyed air conditioning.

- 92 percent of poor households have a microwave.

- Nearly three-fourths have a car or truck, and 31 percent have two or more cars or trucks.

- Nearly two-thirds have cable or satellite TV.

- Two-thirds have at least one DVD player, and 70 percent have a VCR.

- Half have a personal computer, and one in seven have two or more computers.

- More than half of poor families with children have a video game system, such as an Xbox or PlayStation.

- 43 percent have Internet access.

- One-third have a wide-screen plasma or LCD TV.

- One-fourth have a digital video recorder system, such as a TiVo.

In reality, most of the poor do not experience hunger or food shortages.

For decades, the living conditions of the poor have steadily improved. Consumer items that were luxuries or significant purchases for the middle class a few decades ago have become commonplace in poor households, partially because of the normal downward price trend that follows introduction of a new product.

The Reality About Hunger

Liberals use the declining relative prices of many amenities to argue that it is no big deal that poor households have air conditioning, computers, cable TV, and wide-screen TV. They contend, polemically, that even though most poor families may have a house full of modern conveniences, the average poor family still suffers from substantial deprivation in basic needs, such as food and housing. In reality, this is just not true.

Although the mainstream media broadcast alarming stories about widespread and severe hunger in the nation, in reality, most of the poor do not experience hunger or food shortages. The U.S. Department of Agriculture collects data on these topics in its household food security survey. For 2009, the survey showed:

- 96 percent of poor parents stated that their children were never hungry at any time during the year because they could not afford food.

- 83 percent of poor families reported having enough food to eat.

- 82 percent of poor adults reported never being hungry at any time in the prior year due to lack of money for food.

Other government surveys show that the average consumption of protein, vitamins, and minerals is virtually the same for poor and middle-class children and is well above recommended norms in most cases.

The Housing of the Poor

Television newscasts about poverty in America generally portray the poor as homeless people or as a destitute family living in an overcrowded, dilapidated trailer. In fact, however:

- Over the course of a year, 4 percent of poor persons become temporarily homeless.

- Only 9.5 percent of the poor live in mobile homes or trailers, 49.5 percent live in separate single-family houses or townhouses, and 40 percent live in apartments.

- 42 percent of poor households actually own their own homes.

- Only 6 percent of poor households are overcrowded. More than two-thirds have more than two rooms per person.

- The average poor American has more living space than the typical non-poor person in Sweden, France, or the United Kingdom.

- The vast majority of the homes or apartments of the poor are in good repair.

By their own reports, the average poor person had sufficient funds to meet all essential needs and to obtain medical care for family members throughout the year whenever needed.

Anti-poverty policy needs to be based on accurate information.

Of course, poor Americans do not live in the lap of luxury. The poor clearly struggle to make ends meet, but they are generally struggling to pay for cable TV, air conditioning, and a car, as well as for food on the table. The average poor person is far from affluent, but his lifestyle is far from the images of stark deprivation purveyed equally by advocacy groups and the media.

The Need for Accurate Information

The fact that the average poor household has many modern conveniences and experiences no substantial hardships does not mean that no families face hardships. As noted, the overwhelming majority of the poor are well housed and not overcrowded, but one in 25 will become temporarily homeless during the year. While most of the poor have a sufficient and fairly steady supply of food, one in five poor adults will experience temporary food shortages and hunger at some point in a year.

The poor man who has lost his home or suffers intermittent hunger will find no consolation in the fact that his condition occurs infrequently in American society. His hardships are real and must be an important concern for policymakers. Nonetheless, anti-poverty policy needs to be based on accurate information. Gross exaggeration of the extent and severity of hardships in America will not benefit society, the taxpayers, or the poor.

Finally, welfare policy needs to address the causes of poverty, not merely the symptoms. Among families with children, the collapse of marriage and erosion of the work ethic are the principal long-term causes of poverty. When the recession ends, welfare policy must require able-bodied recipients to work or prepare for work as a condition of receiving aid. It should also strengthen marriage in low-income communities rather than ignore and penalize it.

Chapter 2

Do Government Social Assistance Programs Help the Poor?

Overview: The Supplemental Nutrition Assistance Program

Congressional Budget Office

The Congressional Budget Office (CBO) is a nonpartisan agency within the legislative branch of the US government that provides economic analysis to Congress.

The Supplemental Nutrition Assistance Program (SNAP, formerly known as Food Stamps) provides benefits to low-income households to help them purchase food. The program is an "automatic stabilizer," meaning that its number of beneficiaries and amount of spending increase automatically during tough economic times. In fiscal year 2011, total federal expenditures on SNAP—$78 billion—and participation in the program (measured as the number of participants and as a share of the U.S. population) were the highest they have ever been. In an average month that year, nearly 45 million people (or one in seven U.S. residents) received SNAP benefits.

An Increase in SNAP Recipients

The number of people receiving SNAP benefits increased by almost 50 percent between fiscal years 2001 and 2005 and even more rapidly (by 70 percent) between fiscal years 2007 and 2011. During that latter period, spending on SNAP benefits grew by about 135 percent. The increase in the number of people eligible for and receiving benefits between 2007 and 2011 has been driven primarily by the weak economy. That increase was responsible for about 65 percent of the growth in spending on benefits between 2007 and 2011. About 20 percent of the growth in spending can be attributed to temporarily higher benefit amounts enacted in the American Recov-

Congressional Budget Office, "The Supplemental Nutrition Assistance Program," April 2012, pp. 1–5.

ery and Reinvestment Act of 2009 (ARRA). The remainder stemmed from other factors, such as higher food prices and lower income among beneficiaries, both of which boost benefits.

According to the Congressional Budget Office's (CBO's) March 2012 projections, the number of people who receive SNAP benefits will continue to rise slightly from fiscal year 2012 through fiscal year 2014, then decline in the following years. By fiscal year 2022, CBO projects, 34 million people (or about 1 in 10 U.S. residents) will receive SNAP benefits each month (roughly the same as the number in 2009), and SNAP expenditures, at about $73 billion, will be among the highest of all non-health-related federal support programs for low-income households.

Most people receiving SNAP benefits live in households with very low income.

In considering the future of the program, some policymakers might want to scale it back as part of a larger effort to reduce federal spending. Others might want to expand it to provide more assistance to people or to boost the economy in the short term. The current program could be changed by modifying eligibility rules, benefit amounts, administrative procedures, or other program activities, or by converting SNAP to a block grant program.

Characteristics of SNAP Recipients

In fiscal year 2010, the most recent year for which detailed demographic data are available, about three-quarters of households receiving SNAP benefits included a child, a person age 60 or older, or a disabled person. Because households with children tend to be larger, they are likely to receive higher benefits than households without children. The average household receiving benefits consisted of 2.2 people. About half of all households receiving benefits were single-person households.

Most people receiving SNAP benefits live in households with very low income. In fiscal year 2010, 85 percent of households receiving benefits had income (excluding SNAP benefits) below the federal poverty guideline (about $18,500 per year for a household of three). About 30 percent of recipient households reported earned income, and about 60 percent of households reported receiving unearned income from sources including the Supplemental Security Income (SSI) program, Social Security, and the Temporary Assistance for Needy Families (TANF) program. (Some households received both earned and unearned income.)

Over time, the share of SNAP households with earned income and the share with no income have both risen, whereas the share receiving cash assistance from Aid to Families with Dependent Children (AFDC) or its successor, TANF, has declined significantly. In 1990, just under 20 percent of SNAP households had earned income, and fewer than 10 percent reported no income. In 2010, in contrast, the share of households with earned income was roughly 30 percent, and about 20 percent of households reported having no income. In that year, less than 10 percent of households were receiving cash assistance from TANF, compared with more than 40 percent that were receiving cash assistance in 1990 from AFDC. Some of the increase in the share of households with earned income probably occurred because of changes in SNAP's rules and operation that made it easier for people who work to participate in the program. Most of the decline in the share of households receiving SNAP benefits that also received cash assistance was because of an overall reduction in the number of households receiving such assistance.

SNAP benefits represent a significant supplement to income for many households. The average household receiving

SNAP benefits in 2010 had an income of $731 per month (excluding the value of SNAP benefits), or about $8,800 per year. The monthly SNAP benefit per household averaged $287, or $4.30 per person per day. On average, SNAP benefits boosted gross monthly income by 39 percent for all participating households and by 45 percent for households with children.

On average, 45 million people (or about one in seven residents in the United States) received SNAP benefits each month in fiscal year 2011.

People who receive benefits tend to increase their total spending on food. Also, the receipt of SNAP benefits frees up resources that people can use to purchase other items and services. Recent evidence suggests that food security (defined as having access to adequate food for active healthy living) increases in households when they begin receiving benefits. Participation in SNAP may have other consequences for recipients, such as effects on health or nutrition, but evidence has so far been inconclusive. In addition, receipt of SNAP benefits may reduce some people's incentive to work or their willingness to ask for help from family members or informal community networks, although research on those effects over the past 10 to 20 years is scant.

SNAP Participation
and Economic Conditions

The number of people receiving SNAP benefits varies in response to changes in economic conditions. Even without new legislation, the number of beneficiaries rises noticeably during economic downturns. Then, as people's economic situation subsequently improves, some participants leave the program and fewer new households enroll. Nevertheless, participation following an economic downturn does not always drop back to the level experienced before the downturn.

Between 1990 and 2011, the number of SNAP participants increased during periods of relatively high unemployment. Even as the unemployment rate began to decline from its 1992, 2003, and 2010 peaks, decreases in participation typically lagged improvement in the economy by several years. For example, the number of SNAP participants rose steadily from about 20 million in the fall of 1989 to more than 27 million in April 1994—nearly two years after the unemployment rate began to fall and a full three years after the official end of the recession in March 1991. The number of people receiving SNAP benefits began to climb again in 2001 and continued to grow until 2006, more than two years after the unemployment rate began to decline and well after that recession ended (in November 2001). The number of participants temporarily leveled off in 2006 and 2007 until the unemployment rate began to rise sharply in 2008. Participation then started to grow quickly and has continued to increase since then.

The Impact of the Recession

Between 2007 and 2011, the number of people receiving SNAP benefits and federal spending on the program increased significantly. On average, 45 million people (or about one in seven residents in the United States) received SNAP benefits each month in fiscal year 2011. That number represents a dramatic increase over the roughly 26 million people (or 1 of every 11) who received benefits in 2007. The primary reason for the increase in the number of participants was the deep recession from December 2007 to June 2009 and the subsequent slow recovery; there were no significant legislative expansions of eligibility for the program during that time.

Between 2007 and 2011, both the number of people eligible for SNAP and the rate at which eligible people claimed benefits increased. Labor market conditions deteriorated dra-

matically between 2007 and 2009 and have been slow to re-
cover: The unemployment rate jumped from 4.6 percent in
2007 to 9.6 percent in 2010 and was still at 8.5 percent at the
end of 2011. The number of people eligible for the program
increased by an estimated 20 percent from 2007 to 2009 (the
latest year for which such data are available) and probably at
an even faster rate from 2009 to 2011.

Moreover, in 2009, 72 percent of people estimated to be
eligible for SNAP received benefits, up from 69 percent in
2007. Again, the percentage in 2011 was probably greater. The
increase in the rate at which eligible people received SNAP
benefits between 2007 and 2011 was probably a result of two
factors: the poor economy (which reduced people's income
and caused longer periods of need, prompting more people
who were already eligible for the program to apply) and
changes in the program's administration, such as greater use
of online applications, mail-in renewals, and phone interviews
(which have made it easier for people to apply for and continue receiving benefits).

The poorest households were most likely to participate in
the program. Although only 72 percent of people estimated to
be eligible for benefits received them in 2009, a much greater
percentage, an estimated 91 percent, of the benefits that all
eligible people could have received were paid out. Those per-
centages indicate that eligible households that have lower income (and thus qualify for higher benefits) are more likely to
participate in SNAP than eligible households with higher income. (By comparison, in 2001, when the U.S. economy was
much stronger, about 65 percent of the benefits for which
people were eligible were paid out, researchers estimate.)

The Increase in Spending on SNAP

Outlays for SNAP benefits more than doubled between 2007
and 2011, from about $30 billion to $72 billion. Almost two-
thirds of the growth in spending on SNAP benefits between

2007 and 2011 stemmed from the increasing number of participants. Over that five-year period, the number of SNAP participants rose by 70 percent, while spending on benefits grew by about 135 percent.

Spending on benefits grew much faster than the number of SNAP participants for several reasons. About 20 percent of that spending growth was directly attributable to changes in SNAP that were enacted in ARRA, which temporarily boosted the maximum benefits by 13.6 percent relative to 2009 amounts and held them at that level until inflation caught up. (Subsequent legislation imposed an earlier expiration date on those higher benefits.) As a result, the maximum benefit in fiscal year 2009 for households with three members increased from $463 to $526 per month and is scheduled to remain at that amount until the beginning of fiscal year 2014. The remaining increase in total benefits paid was attributable to other factors, such as lower income among beneficiaries and automatic increases in the maximum benefit linked to rising food prices.

The Official Poverty Stats Are Misleading: We're Winning the War on Poverty

Matthew Yglesias

Matthew Yglesias is a business and economics correspondent for Slate *and author of* The Rent Is Too Damn High: What to Do About It, and Why It Matters More than You Think.

"We declared war on poverty," Ronald Reagan famously proclaimed, "and poverty won." And indeed, as measured by the official poverty rate, the United States seems to have made very little progress in curbing poverty. But important new research released this week by Bruce D. Meyer of the University of Chicago and James X. Sullivan of the University of Notre Dame indicates that the official measure is giving us an extremely misleading view. In fact, poverty fell substantially over the past several decades before rising a bit during the Great Recession.

Neither liberals nor conservatives have been eager to embrace this idea—the former to bolster support for new programs and the latter to dismiss the efficacy of what's already been done. But as Meyer pointed out in a talk at the Brookings Institution on Thursday, the way the government measures poverty actually by definition excludes the possibility that public programs are lifting families out of poverty. The truth, when examined correctly, is that we've hit upon a very effective means of waging war on poverty—give money to poor people—and we could make even more progress by doing even more of it.

The official poverty line was created in 1963 by food and nutrition economist Mollie Orshansky and hasn't been updated since.

Her method, though arguably appropriate at the time, is incredibly crude by modern standards. Her idea was to calculate the cost of a nutritionally adequate diet for a given-size family. Then she used the early-'60s rule of thumb that food was about one-third the typical family's budget. So calculate the income needed to prevent malnutrition, triple it, and there's your poverty line.

Needless to say, this has only a hazy relationship with modern living standards. Worse, because at the time there were few government programs designed to help the poor, it refers to income before taxes and cash transfer payments. The formula also neglects to include the value of in-kind public services such as food stamps and Medicaid, and smaller programs like housing vouchers.

The problems with the poverty-line methodology are well known, but they are often thought to impact merely the level of poverty, rather than the change over time. Meyer and Sullivan challenge this assumption. They argue for starters that the standard inflation measure suffers from "outlet bias." It fails, in other words, to adequately account for the rise of cheaper big box stores—exactly the kind of development most likely to benefit the poor. Merely making this inflation adjustment paints a brighter picture of living standards at the low end.

Long-term investment in anti-poverty spending has done exactly what it is supposed to do.

They also show that public policy has made a big difference in the real poverty rate. Throughout the '60s and '70, the tax code was made friendlier to poor people. That was partially rolled back by Ronald Reagan in 1981, but then the 1986 tax reform changed the tide again by introducing the Earned

Income Tax Credit. This important program—a form of wage subsidy for low-income families—pushed after-tax poverty down substantially in the early 1990s. The tax provisions of the 2009 stimulus bill, once again, made the after-tax situation of low-income households better looking than the official line's pretax numbers would suggest. Social Security, especially through its disability insurance function, has also played a big role in pushing actual poverty between 1967 and 2010 down six percentage points more than the official stats say. Other cash transfers—unemployment iInsurance, veterans' benefits, "welfare," workers' comp—aren't as big a deal, but still make a difference to the tune of one percentage point. What's more, these safety net programs also smoothen the business cycle. When you include them in the calculation, poverty doesn't rise as much during recessions or fall as sharply during recoveries.

The authors also show that if you simply ignore income altogether and look at consumption—what people buy—things look even better. It's not entirely clear why this would be. One theory is that people underreport government benefits they receive. Another is that they're underreporting under-the-table income (perhaps to retain eligibility for benefits). Another factor is that consumption measures do a better job of capturing the existence of in-kind provision of social services—public housing, community health centers, and other efforts to give free or discounted goods to the poor. The demographics of poverty look different if you rely on consumption measures rather than income ones—fewer elderly poor and more poor members of married couple households.

Given the demographic split, it seems clear that better data are needed to understand which populations really face the most severe needs. But whether you look at it in terms of consumption or income, the news is good. The impact of the recession aside, we're clearly winning the decades-long war on poverty. We're doing so in part because the economy is evolving in ways that are favorable to the poor, and in part because our government programs are effective. In particular, the not-very-complicated strategy of giving money to the poor through tax credits and Social Security has steadily pushed the poverty rate down over decades, while safety net programs help shelter people from recessions. It's understandable that advocates like to underscore the severity of social problems. But at a time when many voters seem skeptical about the efficacy of government programs it's worth saying that these programs work. Long-term investment in anti-poverty spending has done exactly what it is supposed to do.

Government Programs Prevented a Surge in Poverty from the Recession

Arloc Sherman

Arloc Sherman is a senior researcher for the Center on Budget and Policy Priorities.

Six temporary federal initiatives enacted in 2009 and 2010 to bolster the economy by lifting consumers' incomes and purchases kept nearly 7 million Americans out of poverty in 2010, under an alternative measure of poverty that takes into account the impact of government benefit programs and taxes. These initiatives—three new or expanded tax credits, two enhancements of unemployment insurance, and an expansion of benefits through the Supplemental Nutrition Assistance Program (SNAP, formerly called food stamps)—were part of the 2009 Recovery Act. Congress subsequently extended or expanded some of them.

The Impact of the Temporary Initiatives

To gauge the impacts of these initiatives on poverty, analysts cannot use the official poverty measure because it counts only cash income and does not take refundable tax credits, SNAP benefits, and other non-cash assistance into account. Therefore, we use a poverty measure that adopts recommendations of the National Academy of Sciences (NAS), and that most experts prefer to the traditional poverty measure. Using the NAS measure to analyze newly released Census data for 2010, we find that the six Recovery Act initiatives kept 6.9 million people above the poverty line in 2010:

- Expansions in the Earned Income Tax Credit (EITC) and Child Tax Credit (CTC) kept 1.6 million people out of poverty.

- The Making Work Pay tax credit, which expired at the end of 2010, kept another 1.5 million people out of poverty.

- Expansions in the duration and level of unemployment insurance benefits kept 3.4 million people out of poverty.

- Expansions in SNAP benefits kept 1.0 million people out of poverty.

These initiatives had a wide reach across the population, reaching a majority of American households. The 6.9 million people kept above the poverty line in 2010 included an estimated 2.5 million children, 200,000 seniors, 3.1 million non-Latino whites, 1.3 million non-Latino blacks, and 2.0 million Latinos.

If the government safety net as a whole ... had not existed in 2010, the poverty rate would have been 28.6 percent, nearly twice the actual 15.5 percent.

The six initiatives also reduced the severity of poverty for 32 million of the 47 million people who were poor under this poverty measure in 2010.

Impact on the Non-Poor

Some of the six initiatives targeted low- and moderate-income households broadly, not just people below or near the poverty line. Because of these initiatives:

- 4.0 million people in 2010 had their family disposable

income kept above the equivalent of $50,000 a year for a two-adult, two-child family (adjusted for family size);

- 5.6 million were kept above the equivalent of $40,000;

- 7.8 million were kept above the equivalent of $30,000;

- 6.1 million were kept above the equivalent of $20,000; and

- 2.4 million were kept above the equivalent of $10,000.

These effects are separate from the poverty reduction that resulted from the effects of these and other measures in preventing a deeper economic downturn with a greater loss of jobs. The Congressional Budget Office has estimated that the 2009 Recovery Act preserved or created between 1.0 and 2.9 million jobs through June 2011. The six initiatives examined here contributed to that result by helping to shore up collapsing consumer demand.

In addition to these six provisions enacted in 2009 and 2010, *existing* policies to promote family income kept millions of additional Americans out of poverty in 2010. Under the same NAS poverty measure, the SNAP and unemployment insurance benefits provided under ongoing law (before taking account of the effect of the program expansions examined here) kept more than 3 million and 1 million people out of poverty in 2010, respectively. If the government safety net as a whole (existing policies, as well as the temporary Recovery Act policies) had not existed in 2010, the poverty rate would have been 28.6 percent, nearly twice the actual 15.5 percent.

Determining Poverty Status

The Center [on Budget and Policy Priorities] estimated the impact of six initiatives enacted in early 2009 as part of the Recovery Act, chosen because their effects can be calculated fairly reliably from available survey data. The six are: three federal income tax credits (expansions to the EITC and Child Tax Credit and creation of a new Making Work Pay tax credit), two unemployment insurance provisions (an increase in the number of available weeks of benefits, and an increase in the weekly benefit amount that was in effect through December 2011 but has since ended), and an increase in monthly SNAP benefit levels.

Data are from the nationally representative Current Population Survey, which the Census Bureau uses for both its official and its alternative measures of poverty. To determine poverty status, we used a measure developed by the Census Bureau and Bureau of Labor Statistics that follows the recommendations of the National Academy of Sciences' panel and that most experts prefer to the official poverty measure. The NAS measure differs from the official poverty measure in three significant ways: it counts more income sources, including tax credits and non-cash benefits such as SNAP assistance (the official measure counts only cash income); it subtracts certain expenses that reduce disposable income, including income and payroll taxes and out-of-pocket medical expenditures and work expenses such as child care; and it employs a modestly revised poverty line that is set at $24,267 for a two-adult, two-child family in an average-cost community and that varies with local housing costs and family composition.

Individuals are considered poor if their family's annual income is below the poverty line for a family of their size and age composition living in their locality. Individuals are considered to have been kept above the poverty line by a particular program if their family income *not counting* the benefits from that program is below the poverty line, but their total income—including those benefits—is above the poverty line. . . .

The Impact of Existing Government Programs

This analysis focuses on the six initiatives enacted in 2009 and 2010, which include one new program (the now-expired Making Work Pay tax credit) and five expansions of existing programs (two unemployment insurance expansions, two tax credit expansions, and a SNAP expansion). But assistance provided under *existing* policies to protect family income also had a marked effect in reducing poverty. . . .

The unemployment insurance program as a whole, for example, kept 4.6 million people above the poverty line in 2010, according to the NAS poverty measure:

- An estimated 3.4 million of that 4.6 million was due to expansions that Congress enacted in the Recovery Act and subsequent legislation in 2009 and 2010. (The additional weeks of eligibility kept 3.2 million people out of poverty, while higher weekly benefits kept another 200,000 people out of poverty in 2010.)

- The remaining 1.2 million people kept out of poverty by unemployment insurance were people lifted out of poverty primarily by assistance that unemployment insurance would have provided under pre-2009 law.

In other words, even without the Recovery Act, government safety-net programs would have protected many people from poverty as the economy turned down. Programs such as unemployment insurance are designed to respond quickly and automatically to an increase in the number of households seeking assistance during a recession. (In 2007, prior to the onset of the recession, the unemployment insurance program kept 700,000 people above the NAS poverty line; our estimates suggest that this figure would have risen to close to 1.2 million by 2010 even without the new initiatives.) Likewise, SNAP would have kept over 3 million people above the poverty line in 2010—up from 2.2 million in 2007—even without the expansion in maximum benefits in the 2009 Recovery Act.

Nonetheless, the new initiatives represent a sizable increase in the protection that these programs—and the safety net as a whole—have provided during one of the most severe economic downturns in decades.

The Economic Downturn

Census data show that in 2010, poverty rates without government income assistance of any sort would have been nearly twice as high as they actually were: 28.6 percent rather than 15.5 percent. This shows the impact of public programs, including not only tax credits, unemployment insurance, and SNAP benefits but also Social Security, Supplemental Security Income, veterans' benefits, public assistance (including Temporary Assistance for Needy Families), and housing assistance, among others, and the net effect of the tax system. *Without* government help from the six initiatives highlighted in this analysis, but *with* the rest of the safety net, the poverty rate in 2010 under our NAS measure would have been 17.8 percent in 2010.

Government assistance shielded the incomes and buying power of millions of families and individuals enough to keep them above the poverty line.

The six initiatives brought poverty down further, so that poverty was considerably lower in 2010 than it otherwise would have been.

- Between 2007 and 2010, the number of Americans below the poverty line increased by 2.9 million (from 44.4 million to 47.3 million), based on the NAS poverty line adjusted for inflation, while the poverty rate under this measure rose from 14.9 percent to 15.5 percent.

- Without the six initiatives, the number of people in poverty would have risen by an estimated 9.9 million people since 2007, or more than three times as much, while the poverty rate would have risen to 17.8 percent, or nearly five times as much as it actually rose. . . .

The safety net was responding to the economic downturn even without these six initiatives. In 2007, some 9.5 percent of all Americans were kept above the NAS poverty line by the remainder of the safety net; this is the percentage of people whose incomes were below the poverty line *before* any government benefits were counted but above the poverty line *after* assistance *other than* the six Recovery Act initiatives was counted. And by 2010, the safety net other than the six temporary initiatives was keeping 10.8 percent of Americans out of poverty. This increase in poverty protection as the economy deteriorated largely reflects the increase in assistance provided by unemployment benefits, tax credits, SNAP assistance, and other benefits that respond automatically to increases in the number of low-income people during economic downturns.

The Extent of Poverty

But these automatic increases would not have been enough by themselves to prevent the NAS poverty rate from rising quite substantially. Without the additional assistance provided by the six initiatives, the poverty rate would have increased from 14.9 percent to 17.8 percent between 2007 and 2010, and 6.9 million more people would have become poor than actually did.

These figures indicate that government assistance shielded the incomes and buying power of millions of families and individuals enough to keep them above the poverty line despite the sharpest deterioration in the economy in decades and prevented a much larger increase in poverty than actually occurred (using the alternative poverty measure discussed here). That is no small accomplishment.

It does not mean, of course, that government assistance staved off all, or even most, recession-related hardship. To the contrary. Neither the official poverty rate nor the alternative poverty rate captures the financial losses of families whose incomes dropped from comfortable levels to only slightly above the poverty line, or of working-poor families that lost wages and fell deeper into poverty, or of families whose assets were depleted or wiped out by plummeting home values or a drop in the value of their retirement savings. Nor do these measures capture rising foreclosures and the lack of affordable housing or disruption and anxiety due to job loss.

Social Security Helps to Reduce Poverty Among the Elderly and Disabled

Bernie Sanders

Bernie Sanders has served as US senator from Vermont since 2007.

According to a new poll conducted for *The Hill*, 77 percent of likely voters believe Social Security is in trouble, while just 15 percent believe the program is financially sound.

A Successful Social Program

In fact, Social Security is the most successful social program in American history.

Before Social Security was established 75 years ago, more than half of our elderly population lived in poverty. Because of Social Security, the poverty figure for seniors today is less than 10 percent. Social Security also provides dignified support for millions of widows, widowers, orphans and people with disabilities.

Throughout its history, in good times and bad, Social Security has paid every nickel it owed to every eligible American. As corporations over the last 30 years destroyed the retirement dreams of millions of older workers by eliminating defined-benefit pension plans, Social Security was there paying full benefits. When Wall Street greed and recklessness caused working people to lose billions in retirement savings, Social Security was there paying full benefits.

According to the latest report of the Social Security Administration, the program will be able to pay all of its promised benefits for the next 26 years. After 2037, Social Security will still be able to pay about 78 percent of promised benefits. The nonpartisan Congressional Budget Office has come to a similar conclusion: Social Security will be able to pay full benefits to every eligible recipient until 2039, and after that, it will be able to cover 80 percent of promised benefits.

> *Despite the manufactured hysteria about a crisis, the truth is that Social Security has not contributed one penny to the very serious deficit situation the United States faces.*

A Safe Investment

Although Social Security will be strong for more than a quarter-century, Congress should strengthen it for the longer term. That is why I agree with the president, who has called for raising the cap on taxable income. Today, that cap is at $106,800. No matter how much money you make, Social Security taxes are only deducted on the first $106,800. Removing the cap on incomes of $250,000 or more would make Social Security fully solvent for generations to come.

Even with no change, Social Security has a $2.6 trillion surplus that is projected to grow to more than $4 trillion in 2023. Is this surplus, as some have suggested, just a pile of worthless IOUs? Absolutely not! Social Security rightly invests its surpluses in U.S. Treasury bonds, the safest interest-bearing securities anywhere. These are the same bonds that wealthy investors and China and other foreign countries have purchased. The bonds are backed by the full faith and credit of the U.S. government, which in our long history has never defaulted on its debt obligations. In other words, Social Security investments are safe.

Moreover, despite the manufactured hysteria about a crisis, the truth is that Social Security has not contributed one penny to the very serious deficit situation the United States faces. Social Security is fully funded by the payroll tax that workers and their employers pay. Deficits have ballooned in recent years mainly because of the costs of two wars, tax breaks for the rich, a Medicare prescription drug program written by the insurance and pharmaceutical industries, and the Wall Street bailout—not Social Security.

Attacks on Social Security

For all its success, Social Security faces unprecedented attacks from Wall Street, the Republican Party and a few Democrats. If the American people are not prepared to fight back, the dismantling of Social Security could begin in the very near future.

Rep. Paul Ryan (R-Wis.), the House Budget Committee chairman, wants to partially privatize Social Security, lower its cost-of-living adjustments and drastically cut benefits. An increasing number of his fellow Republicans agree. Rep. Michele Bachmann (R-Minn.), a leader of the Tea Party movement, wants to "wean" everyone except current retirees off Social Security and Medicare.

There are threats on other fronts. A commission established by President [Barack] Obama called for increasing the retirement age to 69, reducing cost-of-living adjustments for today's retirees and deeply reducing benefits for future retirees who make as little as $42,000 a year.

Why is Social Security under attack? First, Wall Street stands to make billions in profits if workers are forced to invest all of their retirement savings in private financial firms. Second, as the increasingly right-leaning Republican Party has become more anti-government, more and more Republicans simply do not believe government has a responsibility to provide retirement benefits to the elderly, or to help those with disabilities.

In my view, maintaining and strengthening Social Security is absolutely essential to the future well-being of our nation.

For 75 years it has successfully provided dignity and support for tens of millions of Americans. Our job is to keep it strong for the next 75 years.

It shouldn't be privatized. Its benefits shouldn't be cut. The retirement age shouldn't be raised.

Social Assistance Spending Fails to Reduce Poverty

Michael Tanner

Michael Tanner is a senior fellow at the Cato Institute and author of The Poverty of Welfare: Helping Others in Civil Society.

O n January 8, 1964, President Lyndon B. Johnson delivered a State of the Union address to Congress in which he declared an "unconditional war on poverty in America." At the time, the poverty rate in America was around 19 percent and falling rapidly. This year [2012], it is reported that the poverty rate is expected to be roughly 15.1 percent and climbing. Between then and now, the federal government spent roughly $12 trillion fighting poverty, and state and local governments added another $3 trillion. Yet the poverty rate never fell below 10.5 percent and is now at the highest level in nearly a decade. Clearly, we have been doing something wrong.

A Vast Array of Welfare Programs

When most Americans think of welfare, they think of the cash benefit program known as Temporary Assistance to Needy Families (TANF), formerly known as Aid to Families with Dependent Children (AFDC). But in reality TANF is only a tiny portion of a vast array of federal government social welfare programs designed to fight poverty. In fact, if one considers those programs that are means-tested (and therefore obviously targeted to low-income Americans) and programs whose legislative language specifically classifies them as anti-poverty programs, there are currently 126 separate federal government programs designed to fight poverty.

Most welfare programs are means-tested programs that provide aid directly to low-income persons in the form of cash, food, housing, medical care, and so forth, with eligibility based on the recipients' income. The remaining programs are either community-targeted programs, which provide aid to communities that are economically distressed or have large numbers of poor people, or categorical programs, which base eligibility for benefits on belonging to a needy or disadvantaged group, such as migrant workers or the homeless. Some welfare programs are well known; some are barely heard of even in Washington.

We are spending more than enough money to fight poverty but not spending it in ways that actually reduce poverty.

In 2011 the federal government spent roughly $668.2 billion on those 126 programs. That represents an increase of more than $193 billion since Barack Obama became president. This is roughly two and a half times greater than any increase over a similar time frame in U.S. history, and it means an increase in means-tested welfare spending of about 2.4 percent of GDP. If one includes state and local welfare spending, government at all levels will spend more than $952 billion this year to fight poverty. To put this in perspective, the defense budget this year, including spending for the wars in Iraq and Afghanistan, totals $685 billion.

Indeed, federal welfare spending alone totals more than $14,848 for every poor man, woman, and child in this country. For a typical poor family of three, that amounts to more than $44,500. Combined with state and local spending, government spends $20,610 for every poor person in America, or $61,830 per poor family of three. Given that the poverty line for that family is just $18,530, we should have theoretically wiped out poverty in America many times over.

Of course no individual is eligible for every program, and many poor people receive nowhere near this amount of funding. And many supposedly anti-poverty programs are poorly targeted, with benefits spilling over to people well above the poverty line. But that is precisely the point—we are spending more than enough money to fight poverty but not spending it in ways that actually reduce poverty. . . .

The 126 Anti-Poverty Programs

The federal government currently funds 126 separate and often overlapping anti-poverty programs. For example, there are 33 housing programs, run by four different cabinet departments, including, strangely, the Department of Energy. There are currently 21 different programs providing food or food-purchasing assistance. These programs are administered by three different federal departments and one independent agency. There are 8 different health care programs, administered by five separate agencies within the Department of Health and Human Services. And six cabinet departments and five independent agencies oversee 27 cash or general assistance programs. All together, seven different cabinet agencies and six independent agencies administer at least one anti-poverty program.

The exact number and composition of these programs fluctuates slightly from year to year, depending on congressional appropriations and presidential priorities. For example, the 2011 federal budget eliminated programs such as the Foster Grandparent Program, the Senior Companion Program, Even Start, and Vista, while creating new ones such as Choice Neighborhood Planning Grants, the Emergency Homeowners Loan Program, and the Capacity Building for Sustainable Communities Fund. However, the number of federal anti-poverty programs has exceeded 100 for more than a decade.

State and local governments provide additional funding for several of these programs and operate a number of programs on their own. Federal spending accounts for roughly two-thirds of welfare funding, with the states—and occasionally localities—accounting for the rest.

The single largest welfare program today is Medicaid. Medicaid spending that supports health care for the poor, excluding funding for nursing home or long-term care for the elderly, topped $228 billion in 2011. The Supplemental Nutrition Assistance Program (food stamps) was the second most expensive welfare program, costing taxpayers nearly $72 billion. Rounding out the top 10 were the Earned Income Tax Credit, Child Tax Credit, Pell Grants, Supplemental Security Income, the State Children's Health Insurance Program, housing vouchers, and TANF.

Any way that you look at it, we are rapidly becoming a society where more and more people rely on the government for their support.

People Who Benefit from Government Programs

At least 106 million Americans receive benefits from one or more of these programs. Again, Medicaid tops the list, with roughly 49 million poor Americans receiving benefits from this program (once again excluding the elderly receiving assistance to pay for long-term care and nursing home care). Second is food stamps; nearly 41 million Americans, about 15 percent of the population, now receive food stamps, the highest number in U.S. history. Looking at the remainder of the 10 most costly programs, all provide benefits to more than 4.5 million Americans.

None of this, of course, includes middle-class entitlements such as Medicare and Social Security, which, while not designed specifically as anti-poverty programs, nevertheless represent transfer payments from the government. Overall, government payouts, including middle-class entitlements, now account for more than a third of all wages and salaries in the United States. Worse, if one includes salaries from government employment, more than half of Americans receive a substantial portion of their income from the government.

Any way that you look at it, we are rapidly becoming a society where more and more people rely on the government for their support.

An Increase in Welfare Spending

By any measure, U.S. welfare spending has increased dramatically since 1965. In constant dollars, federal spending on welfare and anti-poverty programs has risen from $178 billion to $668 billion, a 375 percent increase in constant 2011 dollars, while total welfare spending—including state and local funds—has risen from $256 billion to $908 billion.

Measured as a percentage of GDP [gross domestic product], federal spending increased more than fourfold, from just 0.83 percent of GDP to 4.4 percent. Total welfare spending nearly tripled, from 2.19 percent of GDP to 6 percent.

And, on a per capita basis, that is per poor person, federal spending has risen by more than 900 percent, from $1,625 to $14,848, while total spending rose by a smaller, but still substantial 651 percent, from $3,032 to $19,743.

Over the last decade the increase has been even more rapid. Federal welfare spending increased significantly under the [George W.] Bush administration, but President Obama has thrown money at anti-poverty programs at an unprecedented rate. Since taking office, the Obama administration has increased spending on welfare programs by more than $193 billion.

These numbers are slightly distorted by the inclusion of Medicaid, where expenditures have increased because of the overall rise in health care costs as well as program expansion. However, even excluding Medicaid, spending on means-tested social welfare programs grew by 26 percent from 1990 to 2008—and much more rapidly since then. Expenditures for every program except TANF increased in real terms. The growth of expenditures has been particularly strong for "in-kind" programs, which provide benefits for specific consumption, such as medical care, food, and housing, rather than cash.

The Impact of the Recession

Some of the increase, of course, is clearly due to the recession. Many of these programs are countercyclical, meaning that they automatically expand during economic downturns. However, increases in both participation and spending were greater during this recession than in previous ones. For example, during the 1980–82 recession, enrollment in food stamps increased by only 635,000, and spending rose by just $124 million (in constant 2012 dollars). During the 1990–92 recession and jobless recovery, enrollment increased by 5.2 million, and spending rose by $9.1 billion. During the current recession (over a comparable three-year period), enrollment increased by 12 million people, while spending increased by $30 billion.

Of course, this recession was deeper than those previous ones—unemployment peaked at 9.8 percent during this recession versus 7.8 percent in 1992. But the dramatically larger increase also suggests that part of the program's growth is due to conscious policy choices by this administration to ease eligibility rules and expand caseloads. For example, income limits for eligibility have risen twice as fast as inflation since 2007 and are now roughly 10 percent higher than they were when Obama took office. Moreover, the definition of "categorical eligibility" for the Supplemental Nutrition Assistance Program was expanded substantially in the 2008 farm bill and led to the asset test for eligibility being relaxed, as values of vehicles, retirement accounts, and education savings accounts began to be excluded from the test. Categorical eligibility allows states to declare large numbers of families eligible for food stamps without actually going through the individual eligibility process. Coupled with the fact that Congress allows states to use this determination for families with incomes up to 200 percent of the poverty line, the combination of the two rules allows large numbers of nonpoor persons to qualify.

The poverty rate has remained relatively constant since 1965, despite rising welfare spending.

The same holds true for other welfare programs. For example, the stimulus bill included a provision that created a new "emergency fund" to help states pay for added welfare recipients, with the federal government footing 80 percent of the cost for the new "clients." This was an important change because it undid many of the incentives contained in the 1996 [Bill] Clinton welfare reform, which helped states to reduce welfare rolls. Under the new rules, states that succeed in getting people off welfare lose the opportunity for increased federal funding. And states that make it easier to stay on welfare (by, say, raising the time limit from two years to five) are rewarded with more taxpayer cash. The bill even let states with rising welfare rolls continue to collect their "case-load reduction" bonuses.

According to Obama administration projections, combined federal and state welfare spending will not drop significantly once the economy fully recovers. As we have seen, welfare spending has continued to increase. By 2014 this spending is likely to equal $1 trillion per year and will total $10.3 trillion over the next 10 years. According to these projections, over the next 10 years, federal and state governments will spend $250,000 for every American currently living in poverty, or $1 million for every poor family of four. And that does not include spending under the Patient Protection and Affordable Care Act, which will dramatically increase the number of low-income Americans participating in Medicaid.

Impact on the Poverty Rate

All this spending has not bought an appreciable reduction in poverty. . . . The poverty rate has remained relatively constant since 1965, despite rising welfare spending. In fact, the only appreciable decline occurred in the 1990s, a time of state experimentation with tightening welfare eligibility, culminating in the passage of national welfare reform (the Personal Responsibility and Work Responsibility Act of 1996). And, since 2006, poverty rates have risen despite a massive increase in spending.

Previous analysis of this sort was criticized, with some justification, because traditional poverty measures do not account for the value of noncash welfare benefits. Nor do they account for costs of taxes or employment costs, or the different costs of living in different parts of the country. However, the Census Bureau has now released a new alternative poverty measure which does take both those benefits and expenses into account. This new measure suggests that the real poverty level in the United States could actually be higher than under the traditional measures by roughly 16 percent.

Of course, this does not mean that anti-poverty spending has had no impact. Certainly it could be argued that, without such spending, poverty levels would be even higher. Indeed, the alternative poverty measure suggests that without welfare benefits, poverty rates could exceed 18 percent. However, most of that difference is attributable to the Earned Income Tax Credit. Other programs have only a marginal impact on poverty rates.

There is also some evidence that even if anti-poverty spending failed to lift many people out of poverty, it did reduce the severity of that poverty. According to the alternative poverty measure, for instance, taking into account the full range of welfare benefits received reduces the number of Americans living in extreme poverty—that is below 50 percent of the poverty level—from 6.2 percent to 5.4 percent. These people remained poor, but less poor than before.

Little Return on Spending

Still, given the level of anti-poverty spending, both in the aggregate and on a per capita basis, this amounts to surprisingly little "bang for the buck." Moreover, other studies suggest that the impact of anti-poverty programs on reducing both poverty and deep poverty was actually greater before recent increases in welfare spending. For example, anti-poverty efforts were more effective among single-parent families and the unemployed, groups most at risk for deep poverty, prior to 1985 than in recent years, despite increasing expenditures.

The concept behind how we fight poverty is wrong.

Clearly we are spending more than enough money to have significantly reduced poverty. Yet we haven't. This should suggest that we are doing something wrong. This is not just a question of the inefficiency of government bureaucracies, although the multiplicity of programs and overlapping jurisdictions surely means that there is a lack of accountability within the system.

In addition, whatever the intention behind government programs, they are soon captured by special interests. The nature of government is such that programs are almost always implemented in a way to benefit those with a vested interest in them rather than to actually achieve the programs' stated goals. As economists Dwight Lee and Richard McKenzie among others point out, the political power necessary to transfer income to the poor is power that can be used to transfer income to the nonpoor, and the nonpoor are usually better organized politically and more capable of using political power to achieve their purposes. Among the nonpoor with a vital interest in anti-poverty programs are social workers and government employees who administer the programs and business people, such as landlords and physicians, who are paid to provide services to the poor. Thus, anti-poverty programs are usually more concerned with protecting the prerogatives of the bureaucracy than with actually fighting poverty.

The Current Approach to Fighting Poverty

But more important, the concept behind how we fight poverty is wrong. The vast majority of current programs are focused on making poverty more comfortable—giving poor people more food, better shelter, health care, and so forth—rather than giving people the tools that will help them escape poverty. And we actually have a pretty solid idea of the keys to getting out of and staying out of poverty: (1) finish school; (2) do not get pregnant outside marriage; and (3) get a job, any job, and stick with it.

> For all [our] spending, we have made remarkably little progress in reducing poverty. Indeed, poverty rates have risen in recent years even as spending on anti-poverty programs has increased.

Consider: High school dropouts are roughly three and a half times more likely to end up in poverty than those who complete at least a high school education. If they do find jobs, their wages are likely to be low. Wages for high school dropouts have declined (in inflation-adjusted terms) by 17.5 percent over the past 30 years. At the same time, children growing up in single parent families are four times more likely to be poor than children growing up in two-parent families. Roughly 63 percent of all poor children reside in single-parent families. And only 2.6 percent of full-time workers are poor.

The "working poor" are a small minority of the poor population. Even part-time work makes a significant difference. Only 15 percent of part-time workers are poor, compared with 23.9 percent of adults who do not work.

To jobs, education, and marriage, we can add one more important stepping stone on the road out of poverty—savings and the accumulation of wealth. As Michael Sherraden of Washington University in St. Louis has noted, "for the vast majority of households, the pathway out of poverty is not through consumption, but through saving and accumulation."

Yet with the exception of some education programs such as Pell grants and some job training programs, little of our current welfare state encourages—and much discourages—the behavior and skills that would help them stay in school, avoid unmarried pregnancies, find a job, and save money. All of this suggests that it is far past time to reevaluate our current approach to fighting poverty. Although a comprehensive alternative to our current welfare state is beyond the scope of this paper, it should be clear that we need to focus less on making poverty more comfortable and more on creating the prosperity that will get people out of poverty.

A Better Way to Fight Poverty

The American welfare state is much larger than commonly believed. The federal government alone currently funds and operates 126 different welfare or anti-poverty programs, spending more than $668 billion per year. State and local governments provide additional funding for several of these programs and also operate a number of programs on their own, adding another $284 billion per year. That means that, at all levels, government is spending more than $952 billion per year, just short of the trillion dollar mark.

Yet for all this spending, we have made remarkably little progress in reducing poverty. Indeed, poverty rates have risen in recent years even as spending on anti-poverty programs has increased. All of this suggests that the answer to poverty lies not in the expansion of the welfare state, but in building the habits and creating the conditions that lead to prosperity.

It would make sense therefore to shift our anti-poverty efforts from government programs that simply provide money or goods and services to those who are living in poverty to efforts to create the conditions and incentives that will make it easier for people to escape poverty. Poverty, after all, is the natural condition of man. Indeed, throughout most of human history, man has existed in the most meager of conditions. Prosperity, on the other hand, is something that is created. And we know that the best way to create wealth is not through government action, but through the power of the free market.

Our current $1 trillion War on Poverty is a failure.

That means that if we wish to fight poverty, we should end those government policies—high taxes and regulatory excess—that inhibit growth and job creation. We should protect capital investment and give people the opportunity to start new businesses. We should reform our failed government school system to encourage competition and choice. We should encourage the poor to save and invest.

We all seek a society where every American can reach his or her full potential, where as few people as possible live in poverty, and where no one must go without the basic necessities of life. More importantly we seek a society in which every person can live a fulfilled and actualized life. Shouldn't we judge the success of our efforts to end poverty not by how much charity we provide to the poor but by how few people need such charity?

By that measure, our current $1 trillion War on Poverty is a failure.

Does Government Need to Grow?

Andrew G. Biggs

Andrew G. Biggs is a resident scholar at the American Enterprise Institute.

W*hen it grows faster than the economy's ability to support it, bad things tend to happen.*
Thomas Jefferson thought that "the natural progress of things is for liberty to yield and government to gain ground." Little in recent history shows him to have been wrong.

The 2012 election cemented in place higher spending, increased regulation, and federal control over the health sector. More broadly, from 1900 to 2012, spending by the federal government rose from less than 7 percent of the gross domestic product to over 40 percent. As the population ages and entitlement spending rises, government outlays—financed by rising taxes, expanding debt, or both—will increase only further. Under President Obama's budget, government spending as a share of the economy would be significantly higher than post-World War II norms. Even Representative Paul Ryan's ambitious Roadmap would allow for a small increase in government outlays.

But why?

Does government need to grow in order for the economy to grow? Data from around the world do show that as economies grow, government spending tends to rise even faster. But this isn't to say that big government causes economies to grow: Another explanation is that countries with large economies are simply able to afford larger governments. Economists

Ryan Messmore, the William E. Simon Fellow in Religion and a Free Society at the Heritage Foundation, visited IHN for a firsthand look at its work. He writes:

> "Mary Kay Baker and her colleagues live this personal approach. They refer to the people they serve not as 'clients' or 'cases' but as 'guests.'... Church members volunteer to house these 'guests' in their church buildings, cook and eat dinner with them and play games with their children or help them with homework."

By its very nature, any government program for the poor is removed from the people it serves.

Plenty of other churches and civil groups across the country take a similar approach. Consider the work of the First Baptist Church (FBC) of Leesburg, Fla. FBC has built a ministry village on its campus to help serve the needy. Volunteers and staff step in to assist people who are down and out, from homeless men and pregnant women to abandoned children and drug addicts.

Again, why? "They love Christ, and Christ loved broken people, so they are moved by their love of Christ to serve those he served," says Pastor Emeritus Charles Roesel.

Is it any wonder that groups such as IHN and FBC wind up serving the poor more effectively and efficiently than a waste-filled and impersonal government program? It's not just a job to the men and women who voluntarily pitch in to help their less fortunate neighbors. They're motivated by religious faith, or simply by basic human decency and compassion. And in so doing, they make their country a better place.

Yes, there are dedicated public servants. Many government people care deeply about their "client populations." But by its very nature, any government program for the poor is removed from the people it serves. The people who collect the checks routinely become a name and a number, not a face and a personality. They're a mouth and an outstretched hand, not a mind and a soul.

Take Bob, an alcoholic that FBC helped. Abandoned by his mother as a child, he later learned she adopted two girls. "Since then, I never felt I was worthy of anybody's love," he said. He turned to substance abuse in a vain effort to fill "a huge hole in my heart." FBO didn't just feed him and give him a bed. They worked with him, emotionally and spiritually, to help heal this poor man.

Upon graduating from FBC's program, Bob remarked, "Now I feel worthy of God's love and that makes me able to love others for the first time."

A government program can't do that. Only people can.

Whose job is it to help? It's ours.

CHAPTER 3

How Should Poverty in America Be Addressed?

Chapter Preface

There are several ways for society to deal with the problem of poverty. Some of the suggested solutions may call for government intervention but many do not. At the heart of the debate about whether poverty should be addressed by the government is a disagreement over the cause of poverty. On the one hand, if poverty is caused by a systemic breakdown in the distribution of resources, then government can fix the problem through the redistribution of resources. On the other hand, if poverty is caused by individual failures or by cultural values, then the solution lies in changing the individual or changing the culture.

Government redistribution of resources take place through various welfare programs, including Social Security, Medicare and Medicaid, unemployment insurance, food stamps, and direct welfare payments, providing both cash and noncash support to families and individuals struggling with poverty. Welfare programs, especially direct cash welfare payments, have always been socially controversial and, since the Personal Responsibility and Work Opportunity Reconciliation Act of 1996, have been time limited. The goal of the welfare reform in the 1990s was to discourage lifelong dependency and to require work from welfare recipients after a certain amount of time, thus shifting responsibility for poverty in the direction of the individual.

Proponents of proposed solutions to poverty that do not ask government to transfer wealth claim that fixing the problem requires finding ways to help the poor help themselves. Harvard University professor Michèle Lamont describes the theory of poverty that finds the condition to be a problem of the culture of an individual: "The basic idea is basically that the poor stay in poverty because they have the wrong values, they are stuck in a vicious circle which prevents them from doing the things that would help them improve their situation."[1] Researcher Robert Rector argues that the current culture of poverty in the United States is one without a work ethic and without marriage: "The American work ethic has eroded. Even in the best of economic times, the poor work very little. Worse, marriage has collapsed in low-income communities. At the outset of the War on Poverty, 7 percent of children were born outside marriage; today, the annual rate is 42 percent. The disappearance of marriage is the principal cause of child poverty and welfare dependence today."[2]

Others deny that culture is the primary cause of poverty. Writer Alyssa Battistoni claims, "Poverty is first and foremost a result of structural forces, from economic growth and job opportunities to segregation and discrimination. Structural poverty can shape cultural responses in ways that perpetuate poverty, but the relationship is much more complicated than the 'culture of poverty' thesis implies."[3] Barbara Ehrenreich denies that culture or individual morals are responsible for poverty: "If we look closely enough, we'll have to conclude that poverty is not, after all, a cultural aberration or a character flaw. Poverty is a shortage of money."[4]

The general public seems split on the issue of whether the poor are able to help themselves. A Gallup/USA Today poll taken in May 2012 found that Americans are divided on the issue of opportunities for the poor to help themselves. When asked, "Are you satisfied or dissatisfied with . . . the opportunity for a poor person in this nation to get ahead by working

1. Michèle Lamont, "Reconsidering Culture and Poverty: A Congressional Briefing," May 13, 2010. http://www.aapss.org/news/2010/06/18/reconsidering-culture-and-poverty-a-congressional-briefing.
2. Robert Rector, "The Facts About Poverty in America," *Human Events*, February 7, 2012. http://www.humanevents.com/2012/02/07/the-facts-about-poverty-in-america.
3. Alyssa Battistoni, "The 'Culture of Poverty' Myth Returns," *Salon*, October 22, 2010. http://www.salon.com/2010/10/22/culture_poverty_battistoni.
4. Barbara Ehrenreich, "Michael Harrington and the 'Culture of Poverty,'" *Nation*, April 2, 2012. http://www.thenation.com/article/166831/michael-harrington-and-culture-poverty#.

hard?" 50 percent said they were satisfied, but almost as many—48 percent—said they were dissatisfied.[5] Whether further help for the poor should include government transfer payments, government policy, private charity, or other incentives will continue to be debated as core disagreements remain about the causes of poverty.

5. Lydia Saad, "Majority in U.S. Dissatisfied With Next Generation's Prospects," Gallup, June 4, 2012. http://www.gallup.com/poll/155021/majority-dissatisfied-next -generation-prospects.aspx.

Raising the Minimum Wage Would Help Lower-Income Workers

Doug Hall and David Cooper

Doug Hall is director of the Economic Analysis and Research Network and David Cooper is an economic analyst at the Economic Policy Institute.

Increasing the minimum wage to $9.80 would benefit millions of workers whose characteristics—in terms of their gender, age, race and ethnicity, educational attainment, work hours, family income, and family composition—contradict some prevailing beliefs about minimum-wage workers. In the first year, with an increase from $7.25 to $8.10, nearly 13 million directly and indirectly affected workers would see higher wages. This number would rise to about 20 million workers with the second incremental increase to $8.95 in 2013, and to more than 28 million workers with the third incremental increase to $9.80 in 2014. . . . As detailed later in this [viewpoint], the vast majority of these workers are not teenage part-time workers; rather, most are at least 20 years old, over half work full time, and many are struggling to support their families.

The Demographics of Minimum-Wage Workers

While increasing the minimum wage would have a sizable impact on both men and women, it would disproportionately affect women. That women comprise 54.5 percent of workers

Doug Hall and David Cooper, "How Raising the Federal Minimum Wage Would Help Working Families and Give the Economy a Boost," *Issue Brief*, no. 341, Economic Policy Institute, August 14, 2012, pp. 2–11. Copyright © 2012 by Economic Policy Institute. All rights reserved. Republished with permission.

who would be affected by a potential minimum-wage increase makes it a women's issue. The share of those affected who are women varies somewhat by state, from a low of 49.3 percent in California to a high of 64.4 percent in Mississippi (according to the authors' analysis of Current Population Survey Outgoing Rotation Group microdata). California and Nevada, also at 49.3 percent, are the only states where women do not constitute the majority of those who would benefit.

Minimum-wage workers are older and, as discussed later, have greater family responsibilities than commonly portrayed. The facts do not support the perception of minimum-wage workers as primarily teenagers working for spending money (though even if true, it would not justify paying teens sub-poverty wages).

Instead ... 87.9 percent of workers who would be affected by increasing the federal minimum wage to $9.80 are at least 20 years old. This share varies from a low of 77.1 percent in Massachusetts to 92.4 percent in Florida (and 93.9 percent in the District of Columbia). Thus, in every state, more than three-fourths of workers who would be affected are at least 20 years old.

Data on educational attainment of those who would be affected by a minimum-wage increase ... dispel the misperception of minimum-wage workers as high school students working in low-wage jobs for spending money.

Increasing the minimum wage would substantially benefit both minority and non-minority workers.... Nationally, 56.1 percent of workers who would be affected are non-Hispanic white workers. Nearly a quarter (23.6 percent) are Hispanic, 14.2 percent are black, and 6.1 percent are Asian or of another race or ethnicity.

As one would expect given the country's diverse social and cultural makeup, the racial and ethnic composition of workers affected by increasing the federal minimum wage to $9.80 varies considerably by state (according to an analysis of Current Population Survey Outgoing Rotation Group microdata):

- The Asian/other composition ranges from 0.5 percent in West Virginia to 75.2 percent in Hawaii.

- The black composition ranges from 0.0 percent in Montana to 43.9 percent in Mississippi (and 53.3 percent in the District of Columbia).

- The Hispanic composition ranges from 0.6 percent in Vermont to 58.7 percent in California.

- The white composition ranges from 9.8 percent in Hawaii to 94.7 percent in West Virginia.

Data on educational attainment of those who would be affected by a minimum-wage increase further dispel the misperception of minimum-wage workers as high school students working in low-wage jobs for spending money. In fact, nationally just 22.6 percent of those who would be affected have less than a high school degree, while fully 42.3 percent have some college education, an associate degree, or a bachelors degree or higher.

Among those who would be affected by increasing the minimum wage to $9.80, only 15.0 percent are part-time workers (defined as those who work less than 20 hours per week). More than half (54.1 percent) work full time (35 or more hours per week), while 30.9 percent work between 20 and 34 hours per week. . . .

Southern states generally have a much smaller share of affected workers who work part time. The states with the lowest shares include Texas (8.6 percent), Arkansas (10.0 percent), and Florida (10.4 percent). (The District of Columbia's share stands at 5.8 percent.) States with the highest shares of affected workers who work part time tend to be concentrated in the Northeast, led by Massachusetts (27.0 percent) and Connecticut (26.0 percent). They are followed by Minnesota (25.4 percent), New Hampshire (25.1 percent), and Maine (25.0 percent).

Families Affected by the Minimum Wage

The family income of those who would be affected by a minimum-wage increase is generally low to moderate.... 70.7 percent of affected families have a total family income of less than $60,000, and nearly a quarter (23.6 percent) have total family income of less than $20,000. Among all U.S. families, the median family income in 2010 was $60,395 (according to data from the Current Population Survey).

The share of families affected by increasing the federal minimum wage to $9.80 with family income under $60,000 varies considerably by state, from about half (49.0 percent) in New Hampshire to more than four-fifths (83.1 percent) in Mississippi....

A minimum-wage increase would boost the wages of a diverse multitude of American workers—and would thus have widespread economic benefits.

Those who would be affected by increasing the minimum wage to $9.80 are vital contributors to their families' earnings. Nationally, the average affected worker earns roughly half (49.4 percent) of his or her family's total income.... This percentage varies from a low of 32.4 percent in Connecticut to a high of 59.5 percent in Mississippi.

Nationally, over a quarter (28.0 percent) of those who would be affected by increasing the minimum wage to $9.80 are parents, while over a third (35.8 percent) are married (according to an analysis of Current Population Survey Outgoing Rotation Group microdata). Moreover, of the 76 million children in the United States, over a quarter (28.2 percent) have a parent who would benefit from the proposed federal minimum-wage increase. This percentage varies from 15.2 percent in Vermont (and 11.5 percent in the District of Columbia) to 39.5 percent in Texas. . . . Four other states where over a third of children have a parent who would benefit from the minimum-wage increase include Mississippi (36.7 percent), Oklahoma (35.6 percent), Georgia (33.9 percent), and Idaho (33.7 percent). Of the five states where more than a third of children have an affected parent, all but Idaho had child poverty rates of 25 percent or more in 2011, highlighting the importance of boosting their family incomes by raising the minimum wage.

In short, a minimum-wage increase would boost the wages of a diverse multitude of American workers—and would thus have widespread economic benefits. The following section details the magnitude of these economic effects.

A Tool for Economic Growth

The immediate benefits of a minimum-wage increase are in the boosted earnings of the lowest-paid workers, but its positive effects would far exceed this extra income. Recent research reveals that, despite skeptics' claims, raising the minimum wage does not cause job loss. In fact, throughout the nation, minimum-wage increases would *create* jobs. Like unemployment insurance benefits or tax breaks for low- and middle-income workers, raising the minimum wage puts more money in the pockets of working families when they need it most, thereby augmenting their spending power. Economists generally recognize that low-wage workers are more likely than any other income group to spend any extra earnings immediately on previously unaffordable basic needs or services.

Increasing the federal minimum wage to $9.80 by July 1, 2014, would give an additional $39.7 billion over the phase-in period to directly and indirectly affected workers, who would, in turn, spend those extra earnings. Indirectly affected workers—those earning close to, but still above, the proposed new minimum wage—would likely receive a boost in earnings due to the "spillover" effect, giving them more to spend on necessities.

The hike in the federal minimum wage would create jobs in every state.

This projected rise in consumer spending is critical to any recovery, especially when weak consumer demand is one of the most significant factors holding back new hiring. Though the stimulus from a minimum-wage increase is smaller than the boost created by, for example, unemployment insurance benefits, it is still substantial—and has the crucial advantage of not imposing significant costs on government.

The Economic Stimulus Effect

Showing that raising the minimum wage would be a tool for modest job creation requires an examination of the stimulative effects of minimum-wage increases. Because minimum-wage increases come from employers, we must construct a "minimum-wage increase multiplier" that takes into account the increase in compensation to low-wage workers and the decrease in corporate profits that both occur as a result of minimum-wage increases. Raising the minimum wage means shifting profits from an entity (the employer) that is much less likely to spend immediately to one (the low-wage worker) that is more likely to spend immediately. Thus, increasing the minimum wage stimulates demand for goods and services, leading employers in the broader economy to bring on new staff to keep up with this increased demand.

When economists analyze the net economic stimulus effect of policy proposals (e.g., tax rate changes that boost income for some and reduce it for others), they use a set of widely accepted fiscal multipliers to calculate the total increase in economic activity due to a particular increase in spending. In applying these multipliers, economists generally recognize a direct relationship between increased economic activity and job creation. This analysis assumes that a $115,000 increase in economic activity results in the creation of one new full-time-equivalent job in the current economy.

Using these same standard fiscal multipliers to analyze the jobs impact of an increase in compensation of low-wage workers and decrease in corporate profits that result from a minimum-wage increase, we find that increasing the national minimum wage from $7.25 to $9.80 per hour by July 1, 2014, would result in a net increase in economic activity of approximately $25 billion over the phase-in period and over that period would generate approximately 100,000 new jobs. In fact, the hike in the federal minimum wage would create jobs in every state. . . . Though the resulting employment impact is modest in the context of the millions of workers currently unemployed nationwide, creating tens of thousands of jobs would be a step in the right direction and would boost the economy.

The multiple positive effects that would result from a higher minimum wage are clear.

The Economic Downturn

Examining the positive effects of a minimum-wage increase leads to an overarching discussion of the economic case for increasing the earnings of the lowest-paid workers during an economic downturn. In the current economic climate, nearly everything is pushing against wage growth. With 3.4 unemployed workers for each job opening, employers do not have to offer substantial wages to hire the workers they need, nor do they have to pay substantial wage increases to retain workers. Indeed, between 2009 (when the last minimum-wage increase took place) and 2011 (the most recent year for which data are available), nearly every state experienced wage erosion at the 20th percentile (according to an analysis of Current Population Survey data).

Even conservative economists suggest higher wages might help speed the recovery. American Enterprise Institute scholar Desmond Lachman, a former managing director at Salomon Smith Barney, told *The New York Times*, "Corporations are taking huge advantage of the slack in the labor market—they are in a very strong position and workers are in a very weak position. They are using that bargaining power to cut benefits and wages, and to shorten hours." According to Lachman, that strategy "very much jeopardizes our chances of experiencing a real recovery."

Furthermore, the national unemployment rate currently stands at 8.3 percent and is not expected to return to pre-recession levels for several years. Considering the past year's [2011–2012] sluggish job growth rate, a minimum-wage increase that creates about 100,000 new jobs would help strengthen the recovery.

The multiple positive effects that would result from a higher minimum wage are clear: It would boost the earnings of working families hardest hit by the Great Recession, spur economic growth, and create about 100,000 net new jobs. In an economic climate in which wage increases for the most vulnerable workers are scarce, raising the minimum wage to $9.80 by July 1, 2014, is an opportunity that America's working families cannot afford to lose.

Reducing Income Inequality Is Necessary to Expand Opportunity

Joseph E. Stiglitz

Joseph E. Stiglitz is professor of economics at Columbia University.

America likes to think of itself as a land of opportunity, and others view it in much the same light. But, while we can all think of examples of Americans who rose to the top on their own, what really matters are the statistics: to what extent do an individual's life chances depend on the income and education of his or her parents?

Inequality in America

Nowadays, these numbers show that the American dream is a myth. There is less equality of opportunity in the United States today than there is in Europe—or, indeed, in any advanced industrial country for which there are data.

This is one of the reasons that America has the highest level of inequality of any of the advanced countries—and its gap with the rest has been widening. In the "recovery" of 2009–2010, the top 1% of US income earners captured 93% of the income growth. Other inequality indicators—like wealth, health, and life expectancy—are as bad or even worse. The clear trend is one of concentration of income and wealth at the top, the hollowing out of the middle, and increasing poverty at the bottom.

It would be one thing if the high incomes of those at the top were the result of greater contributions to society, but the

Joseph E. Stiglitz, "The Price of Inequality," Project Syndicate, June 5, 2012. Copyright © 2012 by Project Syndicate. All rights reserved. Republished with permission.

Great Recession showed otherwise: even bankers who had led the global economy, as well as their own firms, to the brink of ruin, received outsize bonuses.

Americans today are worse off—with lower real (inflation-adjusted) incomes—than they were in 1997, a decade and a half ago. All of the benefits of growth have gone to the top.

A closer look at those at the top reveals a disproportionate role for rent-seeking [using one's resources to increase one's wealth without increasing one's productivity]: some have obtained their wealth by exercising monopoly power; others are CEOs [chief executive officers] who have taken advantage of deficiencies in corporate governance to extract for themselves an excessive share of corporate earnings; and still others have used political connections to benefit from government munificence—either excessively high prices for what the government buys (drugs), or excessively low prices for what the government sells (mineral rights).

Likewise, part of the wealth of those in finance comes from exploiting the poor, through predatory lending and abusive credit-card practices. Those at the top, in such cases, are enriched at the direct expense of those at the bottom.

The Truth About Trickle-Down Economics

It might not be so bad if there were even a grain of truth to trickle-down economics—the quaint notion that everyone benefits from enriching those at the top. But most Americans today are worse off—with lower real (inflation-adjusted) incomes—than they were in 1997, a decade and a half ago. All of the benefits of growth have gone to the top.

Defenders of America's inequality argue that the poor and those in the middle shouldn't complain. While they may be getting a smaller share of the pie than they did in the past, the pie is growing so much, thanks to the contributions of the rich and superrich, that the *size* of their slice is actually larger. The evidence, again, flatly contradicts this. Indeed, America grew far faster in the decades after World War II, when it was growing together, than it has since 1980, when it began growing apart.

This shouldn't come as a surprise, once one understands the sources of inequality. Rent-seeking distorts the economy. Market forces, of course, play a role, too, but markets are shaped by politics; and, in America, with its quasi-corrupt system of campaign finance and its revolving doors between government and industry, politics is shaped by money.

Inequality leads to lower growth and less efficiency.

For example, a bankruptcy law that privileges derivatives over all else, but does not allow the discharge of student debt, no matter how inadequate the education provided, enriches bankers and impoverishes many at the bottom. In a country where money trumps democracy, such legislation has become predictably frequent.

The High Price of Inequality

But growing inequality is not inevitable. There are market economies that are doing better, both in terms of both GDP [gross domestic product] growth and rising living standards for most citizens. Some are even reducing inequalities.

America is paying a high price for continuing in the opposite direction. Inequality leads to lower growth and less efficiency. Lack of opportunity means that its most valuable asset—its people—is not being fully used. Many at the bottom, or even in the middle, are not living up to their potential, because the rich, needing few public services and worried that a strong government might redistribute income, use their political influence to cut taxes and curtail government spending.

This leads to underinvestment in infrastructure, education, and technology, impeding the engines of growth.

The Great Recession has exacerbated inequality, with cutbacks in basic social expenditures and with high unemployment putting downward pressure on wages. Moreover, the United Nations Commission of Experts on Reforms of the International Monetary and Financial System, investigating the causes of the Great Recession, and the International Monetary Fund have both warned that inequality leads to economic instability.

But, most importantly, America's inequality is undermining its values and identity. With inequality reaching such extremes, it is not surprising that its effects are manifest in every public decision, from the conduct of monetary policy to budgetary allocations. America has become a country not "with justice for all," but rather with favoritism for the rich and justice for those who can afford it—so evident in the foreclosure crisis, in which the big banks believed that they were too big not only to fail, but also to be held accountable.

America can no longer regard itself as the land of opportunity that it once was. But it does not have to be this way: it is not too late for the American dream to be restored.

Reducing Income Inequality Will Not Necessarily Help the Poor Be More Economically Mobile

James Q. Wilson

James Q. Wilson is the Ronald Reagan Professor of Public Policy at Pepperdine University.

There is no doubt that incomes are unequal in the United States—far more so than in most European nations. This fact is part of the impulse behind the Occupy Wall Street movement, whose members claim to represent the 99 percent of us against the wealthiest 1 percent. It has also sparked a major debate in the Republican presidential race, where former Massachusetts governor Mitt Romney has come under fire for his tax rates and his career as the head of a private-equity firm.

And economic disparity was the recurring theme of President [Barack] Obama's State of the Union address on Tuesday [January 24, 2012]. "We can either settle for a country where a shrinking number of people do really well, while a growing number of Americans barely get by," the president warned, "or we can restore an economy where everyone gets a fair shot and everyone does their fair share."

The Ever-Changing Rich

But the mere existence of income inequality tells us little about what, if anything, should be done about it. First, we must answer some key questions. Who constitutes the prosperous and the poor? Why has inequality increased? Does an unequal income distribution deny poor people the chance to buy what they want? And perhaps most important: How do Americans feel about inequality?

To answer these questions, it is not enough to take a snapshot of our incomes; we must instead have a motion picture of them and of how people move in and out of various income groups over time.

The "rich" in America are not a monolithic, unchanging class. A study by Thomas A. Garrett, economist at the Federal Reserve Bank of St. Louis, found that less than half of people in the top 1 percent in 1996 were still there in 2005. Such mobility is hardly surprising: A business school student, for instance, may have little money and high debts, but nine years later he or she could be earning a big Wall Street salary and bonus.

Mobility is not limited to the top-earning households. A study by economists at the Federal Reserve Bank of Minneapolis found that nearly half of the families in the lowest fifth of income earners in 2001 had moved up within six years. Over the same period, more than a third of those in the highest fifth of income-earners had moved down. Certainly, there are people such as Warren Buffett and Bill Gates who are ensconced in the top tier, but far more common are people who are rich for short periods.

The real income problem in this country is not a question of who is rich, but rather of who is poor.

The Features of the Rich and Poor

And who are the rich? Affluent people, compared with poor ones, tend to have greater education and spouses who work full time. The past three decades have seen significant increases in real earnings for people with advanced degrees. The

Bureau of Labor Statistics found that between 1979 and 2010, hourly wages for men and women with at least a college degree rose by 33 percent and 20 percent, respectively, while they fell for all people with less than a high school diploma—by 9 percent for women and 31 percent for men.

Also, households with two earners have seen their incomes rise. This trend is driven in part by women's increasing workforce participation, which doubled from 1950 to 2005 and which began to place women in well-paid jobs by the early 1980s.

We could reduce income inequality by trying to curtail the financial returns of education and the number of women in the workforce—but who would want to do that?

The real income problem in this country is not a question of who is rich, but rather of who is poor. Among the bottom fifth of income earners, many people, especially men, stay there their whole lives. Low education and unwed motherhood only exacerbate poverty, which is particularly acute among racial minorities. Brookings Institution economist Scott Winship has argued that two-thirds of black children in America experience a level of poverty that only 6 percent of white children will ever see, calling it a "national tragedy."

The country has become more prosperous, as measured not by income but by consumption.

Making the poor more economically mobile has nothing to do with taxing the rich and everything to do with finding and implementing ways to encourage parental marriage, teach the poor marketable skills and induce them to join the legitimate workforce. It is easy to suppose that raising taxes on the rich would provide more money to help the poor. But the problem facing the poor is not too little money, but too few skills and opportunities to advance themselves.

Poverty in America

Income inequality has increased in this country and in practically every European nation in recent decades. The best measure of that change is the Gini index, named after the Italian statistician Corrado Gini, who designed it in 1912. The index values vary between zero, when everyone has exactly the same income, and 1, when one person has all of the income and everybody else has none. In mid-1970s America, the index was 0.316, but it had reached 0.378 by the late 2000s. One of the few nations to see its Gini value fall was Greece, which went from 0.413 in the 1970s to 0.307 in the late 2000s. So Greece seems to be reducing income inequality—but with little to buy, riots in the streets and economic opportunity largely limited to those partaking in corruption, the nation is hardly a model for anyone's economy.

Poverty in America is certainly a serious problem, but the plight of the poor has been moderated by advances in the economy. Between 1970 and 2010, the net worth of American households more than doubled, as did the number of television sets and air-conditioning units per home. In his book *The Poverty of the Poverty Rate*, Nicholas Eberstadt shows that over the past 30 or so years, the percentage of low-income children in the United States who are underweight has gone down, the share of low-income households lacking complete plumbing facilities has declined, and the area of their homes adequately heated has gone up. The fraction of poor households with a telephone, a television set and a clothes dryer has risen sharply.

In other words, the country has become more prosperous, as measured not by income but by consumption: In constant dollars, consumption by people in the lowest quintile rose by more than 40 percent over the past four decades.

Income as measured by the federal government is not a reliable indicator of well-being, but consumption is. Though poverty is a problem, it has become less of one.

Americans' Attitudes About Income Inequality

Historically, Americans have had an unusual attitude toward income inequality. In 1985, political scientists Sidney Verba and Gary Orren published a book that compared how liberals in Sweden and in the United States viewed such inequality. By four or five to one, the Swedish liberals were more likely than the American ones to believe that it was important to give workers equal pay. The Swedes were three times more likely than the Americans to favor putting a top limit on incomes. (The Swedes get a lot of what they want: Their Gini index is 0.259, much lower than America's.)

Sweden has maintained a low Gini index in part by having more progressive tax rates. If Americans wanted to follow the Swedish example, they could. But what is the morally fair way to determine tax rates—other than taxing everyone at the same rate? The case for progressive tax rates is far from settled; just read Kip Hagopian's recent essay in *Policy Review*, which makes a powerful argument against progressive taxation because it fails to take into account aptitude and work effort.

Reducing poverty, rather than inequality, is also a difficult task, but at least the end is clearer.

American views about inequality have not changed much in the past quarter-century. In their 2009 book *Class War? What Americans Really Think About Economic Inequality*, political scientists Benjamin Page and Lawrence Jacobs report that big majorities, including poor people, agree that "it is 'still possible' to start out poor in this country, work hard, and become rich," and reject the view that it is the government's job to narrow the income gap. More recently, a December [2011] Gallup poll showed that 52 percent of Americans say inequality is "an acceptable part" of the nation's economic system, compared with 45 percent who deemed it a "problem that needs to be fixed." Similarly, 82 percent said economic growth is "extremely important" or "very important," compared with 46 percent saying that reducing the gap between rich and poor is extremely or very important.

Suppose we tax the rich more heavily—who would get the money, and for what goals?

The Social Impact Bond Model

Reducing poverty, rather than inequality, is also a difficult task, but at least the end is clearer. One new strategy for helping the poor improve their condition is known as the "social impact bond," which is being tested in Britain and has been endorsed by the Obama administration. Under this approach, private investors, including foundations, put up money to pay for a program or initiative to help low-income people get jobs, stay out of prison or remain in school, for example. A government agency evaluates the results. If the program is succeeding, the agency reimburses the investors; if not, they get no government money.

As Harvard economist Jeffrey Liebman has pointed out, for this system to work there must be careful measures of success and a reasonable chance for investors to make a profit. Massachusetts is ready to try such an effort. It may not be easy for the social impact bond model to work consistently, but it offers one big benefit: Instead of carping about who is rich, we would be trying to help people who are poor.

The State of Poverty in America

Peter Edelman

Peter Edelman is a law professor at Georgetown University Law Center and faculty director of its Center on Poverty, Inequality, and Public Policy.

The problem is worse than we thought, but we can solve it.

We have two basic poverty problems in the United States. One is the prevalence of low-wage work. The other concerns those who have almost no work.

The two overlap.

Most people who are poor work as much as they can and go in and out of poverty. Fewer people have little or no work on a continuing basis, but they are in much worse straits and tend to stay poor from one generation to the next.

The numbers in both categories are stunning.

Low-wage work encompasses people with incomes below twice the poverty line—not poor but struggling all the time to make ends meet. They now total 103 million, which means that fully one-third of the population has an income below what would be $36,000 for a family of three.

In the bottom tier are 20.5 million people—6.7 percent of the population—who are in deep poverty, with an income less than half the poverty line (below $9,000 for a family of three). Some 6 million people out of those 20.5 million have no income at all other than food stamps.

These dire facts tempt one to believe that there may be some truth to President Ronald Reagan's often-quoted declaration that "we fought a war against poverty and poverty won." But that is not the case. Our public policies have been remarkably successful. Starting with the Social Security Act of 1935, continuing with the burst of activity in the 1960s, and on from there, we have made great progress.

We enacted Medicaid and the Children's Health Insurance Program, and many health indicators for low-income people improved. We enacted food stamps, and the near-starvation conditions we saw in some parts of the country were ameliorated. We enacted the Earned Income Tax Credit and the Child Tax Credit, and the incomes of low-wage workers with children were lifted. We enacted Pell grants, and millions of people could afford college who otherwise couldn't possibly attend. We enacted Supplemental Security Income and thereby raised the income floor for elderly and disabled people whose earnings from work didn't provide enough Social Security. There is much more—housing vouchers, Head Start, child-care assistance, and legal services for the poor, to name a few. The Obama administration and Congress added 16 million people to Medicaid in the Affordable Care Act, appropriated billions to improve the education of low-income children, and spent an impressive amount on the least well-off in the Recovery Act.

We have become a low-wage economy to a far greater extent than we realize.

All in all, our various public policies kept a remarkable 40 million people from falling into poverty in 2010—about half because of Social Security and half due to the other programs just mentioned. To assert that we fought a war against poverty and poverty won because there is still poverty is like saying that the Clean Air and Clean Water acts failed because there is still pollution.

Nonetheless, the level of poverty in the nation changed little between 1970 and 2000 and is much worse now. It was at 11.1 percent in 1973—the lowest level achieved since we began measuring—and after going up sharply during the Reagan and George H.W. Bush years, went back down during the 1990s to 11.3 percent in 2000, as President Bill Clinton left office.

Why didn't it fall further? The economics have been working against us for four decades, exacerbated by trends in family composition. Well-paying industrial jobs disappeared to other countries and to automation. The economy grew, but the fruits of the growth went exclusively to those at the top. Other jobs replaced the ones lost, but most of the new jobs paid much less. The wage of the median-paying job barely grew—by one measure going up only about 7 percent over the 38 years from 1973 to 2011. Half the jobs in the country now pay less than $33,000 a year, and a quarter pay less than the poverty line of $22,000 for a family of four. We have become a low-wage economy to a far greater extent than we realize.

Households with only one wage-earner—typically those headed by single mothers—have found it extremely difficult to support a family. The share of families with children headed by single mothers rose from 12.8 percent in 1970 to 26.2 percent in 2010 (and from 37.1 percent in 1971 to 52.8 percent in 2010 among African Americans). In 2010, 46.9 percent of children under 18 living in households headed by a single mother were poor.

The percentage of people in deep poverty has doubled since 1976. A major reason for this rise is the near death of cash assistance for families with children. Welfare has shrunk from 14 million recipients (too many, in my view) before the Temporary Assistance for Needy Families law (TANF) was enacted in 1996 to 4.2 million today, just 1.5 percent of the population. At last count, Wyoming had 607 people on TANF, or just 2.7 percent of its poor children. Twenty-six states have less than 20 percent of their poor children on TANF. The proportion of poor families with children receiving welfare has shrunk from 68 percent before TANF was enacted to 27 percent today.

We have to restore the safety net for the poorest of the poor.

What's the agenda going forward? The heart of it is creating jobs that yield a living income. Restoring prosperity, ensuring that the economy functions at or near full employment, is our most powerful anti-poverty weapon. We need more, though—a vital union sector and a higher minimum wage, for two. We also need work supports—health care, child care, and help with the cost of housing and postsecondary education. These are all income equivalents—all policies that will contribute to bringing everyone closer to having a living income.

There's a gigantic problem here, however: We look to be headed to a future of too many low-wage jobs. Wages in China, India, and other emerging economies may be rising, but we can't foresee any substantial increase in the prevailing wage for many millions of American jobs. That means we better start talking about wage supplements that are much bigger than the Earned Income Tax Credit. We need a dose of reality about the future of the American paycheck.

The second big problem is the crisis—and it is a crisis—posed by the 20 million people at the bottom of the economy. We have a huge hole in our safety net. In many states, TANF and food stamps combined don't even get people to half of the poverty line, and a substantial majority of poor families don't receive TANF at all.

Even worse, we have destroyed the safety net for the poorest children in the country. Seven million women and children are among the 20.5 million in deep poverty. One in four children in a household headed by a single mother is in deep poverty. We have to restore the safety net for the poorest of the poor.

Getting serious about investing in our children—from prenatal care and early-childhood assistance on through education at all levels—is also essential if we are to achieve a future without such calamitous levels of poverty. In addition, we must confront the destruction being wrought by the criminal-justice system. These are poverty issues and race issues as well. The schools and the justice system present the civil-rights challenges of this century.

Combining all of the problems in vicious interaction is the question of place—the issues that arise from having too many poor people concentrated in one area, whether in the inner city, Appalachia, the Mississippi Delta, or on Indian reservations. Such places are home to a minority of the poor, but they include a hugely disproportionate share of intergenerational and persistent poverty. Our most serious policy failing over the past four-plus decades has been our neglect of this concentrated poverty. We have held our own in other respects, but we have lost ground here.

Finally, we need to be much more forthright about how much all of this has to do with race and gender. It is always important to emphasize that white people make up the largest number of the poor, to counter the stereotype that the face of poverty is one of color. At the same time, though, we must face more squarely that African Americans, Latinos, and Native Americans are all poor at almost three times the rate of whites and ask why that continues to be true. We need as a nation to be more honest about who it is that suffers most from terrible schools and the way we lock people up. Poverty most definitely cuts across racial lines, but it doesn't cut evenly.

There's a lot to do.

Why Capitalism Has an Image Problem

Charles Murray

Charles Murray is the W.H. Brady Scholar at the American Enterprise Institute and author of Coming Apart: The State of White America, 1960–2010.

Charles Murray examines the cloud now hanging over American business—and what today's capitalists can do about it.

Mitt Romney's résum´e at Bain should be a slam dunk. He has been a successful capitalist, and capitalism is the best thing that has ever happened to the material condition of the human race. From the dawn of history until the 18th century, every society in the world was impoverished, with only the thinnest film of wealth on top. Then came capitalism and the Industrial Revolution. Everywhere that capitalism subsequently took hold, national wealth began to increase and poverty began to fall. Everywhere that capitalism didn't take hold, people remained impoverished. Everywhere that capitalism has been rejected since then, poverty has increased.

Capitalism has lifted the world out of poverty because it gives people a chance to get rich by creating value and reaping the rewards. Who better to be president of the greatest of all capitalist nations than a man who got rich by being a brilliant capitalist?

Yet it hasn't worked out that way for Mr. Romney. "Capitalist" has become an accusation. The creative destruction that is at the heart of a growing economy is now seen as evil. Americans increasingly appear to accept the mind-set that kept the world in poverty for millennia: If you've gotten rich, it is because you made someone else poorer.

What happened to turn the mood of the country so far from our historic celebration of economic success?

Two important changes in objective conditions have contributed to this change in mood. One is the rise of collusive capitalism. Part of that phenomenon involves crony capitalism, whereby the people on top take care of each other at shareholder expense (search on "golden parachutes").

It looks to a large proportion of the public as if we've got some fabulously wealthy people who haven't done anything to deserve their wealth.

But the problem of crony capitalism is trivial compared with the collusion engendered by government. In today's world, every business's operations and bottom line are affected by rules set by legislators and bureaucrats. The result has been corruption on a massive scale. Sometimes the corruption is retail, whereby a single corporation creates a competitive advantage through the cooperation of regulators or politicians (search on "earmarks"). Sometimes the corruption is wholesale, creating an industrywide potential for profit that would not exist in the absence of government subsidies or regulations (like ethanol used to fuel cars and low-interest mortgages for people who are unlikely to pay them back). Collusive capitalism has become visible to the public and increasingly defines capitalism in the public mind.

Another change in objective conditions has been the emergence of great fortunes made quickly in the financial markets. It has always been easy for Americans to applaud people who get rich by creating products and services that people want to buy. That is why Thomas Edison and Henry Ford were American heroes a century ago, and Steve Jobs was one when he died last year.

When great wealth is generated instead by making smart buy and sell decisions in the markets, it smacks of inside knowledge, arcane financial instruments, opportunities that aren't accessible to ordinary people, and hocus-pocus. The good that these rich people have done in the process of getting rich is obscure. The benefits of more efficient allocation of capital are huge, but they are really, really hard to explain simply and persuasively. It looks to a large proportion of the public as if we've got some fabulously wealthy people who haven't done anything to deserve their wealth.

The objective changes in capitalism as it is practiced plausibly account for much of the hostility toward capitalism. But they don't account for the unwillingness of capitalists who are getting rich the old-fashioned way—earning it—to defend themselves.

Capitalism's reputation has fallen on hard times and the principled case for capitalism must be made anew.

I assign that timidity to two other causes. First, large numbers of today's successful capitalists are people of the political left who may think their own work is legitimate but feel no allegiance to capitalism as a system or kinship with capitalists on the other side of the political fence. Furthermore, these capitalists of the left are concentrated where it counts most. The most visible entrepreneurs of the high-tech industry are predominantly liberal. So are most of the people who run the entertainment and news industries. Even leaders of the financial industry increasingly share the politics of George Soros. Whether measured by fundraising data or by the members of Congress elected from the ZIP Codes where they live, the elite centers with the most clout in the culture are filled with people who are embarrassed to identify themselves as capitalists, and it shows in the cultural effect of their work.

Another factor is the segregation of capitalism from virtue. Historically, the merits of free enterprise and the obligations of success were intertwined in the national catechism. McGuffey's Readers, the books on which generations of American children were raised, have plenty of stories treating initiative, hard work and entrepreneurialism as virtues, but just as many stories praising the virtues of self-restraint, personal integrity and concern for those who depend on you. The freedom to act and a stern moral obligation to act in certain ways were seen as two sides of the same American coin. Little of that has survived.

To accept the concept of virtue requires that you believe some ways of behaving are right and others are wrong always and everywhere. That openly judgmental stand is no longer acceptable in America's schools nor in many American homes. Correspondingly, we have watched the deterioration of the sense of stewardship that once was so widespread among the most successful Americans and the near disappearance of the sense of seemliness that led successful capitalists to be obedient to unenforceable standards of propriety. Many senior figures in the financial world were appalled by what was going on during the run-up to the financial meltdown of 2008. Why were they so silent before and after the catastrophe? Capitalists who behave honorably and with restraint no longer have either the platform or the vocabulary to preach their own standards and to condemn capitalists who behave dishonorably and recklessly.

And so capitalism's reputation has fallen on hard times and the principled case for capitalism must be made anew. That case has been made brilliantly and often in the past, with Milton Friedman's *Capitalism and Freedom* being my own favorite. But in today's political climate, updating the case for capitalism requires a restatement of old truths in ways that Americans from across the political spectrum can accept. Here is my best effort:

The U.S. was created to foster human flourishing. The means to that end was the exercise of liberty in the pursuit of happiness. Capitalism is the economic expression of liberty. The pursuit of happiness, with happiness defined in the classic sense of justified and lasting satisfaction with life as a whole, depends on economic liberty every bit as much as it depends on other kinds of freedom.

"Lasting and justified satisfaction with life as a whole" is produced by a relatively small set of important achievements that we can rightly attribute to our own actions. Arthur Brooks, my colleague at the American Enterprise Institute, has usefully labeled such achievements "earned success." Earned success can arise from a successful marriage, children raised well, a valued place as a member of a community, or devotion to a faith. Earned success also arises from achievement in the economic realm, which is where capitalism comes in.

Earning a living for yourself and your family through your own efforts is the most elemental form of earned success. Successfully starting a business, no matter how small, is an act of creating something out of nothing that carries satisfactions far beyond those of the money it brings in. Finding work that not only pays the bills but that you enjoy is a crucially important resource for earned success.

Making a living, starting a business and finding work that you enjoy all depend on freedom to act in the economic realm. What government can do to help is establish the rule of law so that informed and voluntary trades can take place. More formally, government can vigorously enforce laws against the use of force, fraud and criminal collusion, and use tort law to hold people liable for harm they cause others.

Everything else the government does inherently restricts economic freedom to act in pursuit of earned success. I am a libertarian and think that almost none of those restrictions are justified. But accepting the case for capitalism doesn't require you to be a libertarian. You are free to argue that certain

government interventions are justified. You just need to acknowledge this truth: Every intervention that erects barriers to
starting a business, makes it expensive to hire or fire employees, restricts entry into vocations, prescribes work conditions
and facilities, or confiscates profits interferes with economic
liberty and usually makes it more difficult for both employers
and employees to earn success. You also don't need to be a
libertarian to demand that any new intervention meet this
burden of proof: It will accomplish something that tort law
and enforcement of basic laws against force, fraud and collusion do not accomplish.

*Freeing capitalism to do what it does best won't just cre-
ate national wealth and reduce poverty, but expand the
ability of Americans to achieve earned success.*

People with a wide range of political views can also acknowledge that these interventions do the most harm to individuals and small enterprises. Huge banks can, albeit at great
expense, cope with the Dodd-Frank law's absurd regulatory
burdens; many small banks cannot. Huge corporations can
cope with the myriad rules issued by the Occupational Safety
and Health Administration, the Environmental Protection
Agency, the Equal Employment Opportunity Commission and
their state-level counterparts. The same rules can crush small
businesses and individuals trying to start small businesses.

Finally, people with a wide range of political views can acknowledge that what has happened incrementally over the
past half-century has led to a labyrinthine regulatory system,
irrational liability law and a corrupt tax code. Sweeping sim-
plifications and rationalizations of all these systems are possible in ways that even moderate Democrats could accept in a
less polarized political environment.

To put it another way, it should be possible to revive a national consensus affirming that capitalism embraces the best

and most essential things about American life; that freeing capitalism to do what it does best won't just create national wealth and reduce poverty, but expand the ability of Americans to achieve earned success—to pursue happiness.

Reviving that consensus also requires us to return to the vocabulary of virtue when we talk about capitalism. Personal integrity, a sense of seemliness and concern for those who depend on us are not "values" that are no better or worse than other values. Historically, they have been deeply embedded in the American version of capitalism. If it is necessary to remind the middle class and working class that the rich are not their enemies, it is equally necessary to remind the most successful among us that their obligations are not to be measured in terms of their tax bills. Their principled stewardship can nurture and restore our heritage of liberty. Their indifference to that heritage can destroy it.

Marriage Is a Solution to Ending Poverty

Robert Rector and Rachel Sheffield

Robert Rector is a senior research fellow and Rachel Sheffield a research associate at the Heritage Foundation.

Poverty and inequality in America are hot topics these days, and not just among the Occupy Wall Street crowd. Yet amid all the chatter, hardly anyone talks about the greatest driver of poverty: the rapidly rising number of babies born to unmarried mothers.

Births Outside Marriage

Today, over 40 percent of U.S. births—four in 10—occur outside marriage. In 1960, it was below one in 10. The trend isn't limited to just a few states, either.

All states, including Arkansas, have seen similar trends, as illustrated by a new Heritage Foundation report based on data from the U.S. Census Bureau. Sadly, in Arkansas the number of children born to single mothers—nearly 46 percent—is higher than the national average.

Couple this trend with the finding that children born outside marriage are roughly five times as likely to be poor as those born to married parents, and we have a recipe for economic disaster.

Although births to unwed mothers often are attributed to teens, less than 10 percent of all unwed births in America overall, as well as in Arkansas, are to women under 18. Roughly 80 percent of out-of-wedlock births are to women between 18 and 29, and most often their formal education went no further than a high school diploma.

Rather than a teen issue, then, the rise in childbearing outside marriage springs from a breakdown of relationships among young adult men and women in low-income communities.

A Two-Caste System

Yet, it isn't because these men and women don't value marriage. In fact, just the opposite is true. Marriage is valued so highly in low-income populations that it has become a crowning event—a ceremony symbolizing arrival into the middle class—rather than a crucial pathway leading to the attainment of middle-class status. Having children—also extremely valued—occurs on the pathway to marriage, not afterward.

Marriage decreases poverty at all education levels.

Unlike their college-educated counterparts who wait until after marriage to have children, these young adults are doing the exact opposite. Poverty, a string of unstable relationships and huge welfare costs to the taxpayer are the results.

This difference in marriage and childbearing patterns between low-income young adults and their educated peers has led to a society that is steadily splitting into a two-caste system—with marriage and education as the dividing line. In the higher-income third of the population, children are raised by college-educated, married parents; in the lower-income third, children are raised by single parents with no more than a high school education.

Indeed, marriage decreases poverty at all education levels. The effectiveness of marriage in preventing poverty is the equivalent of adding five to six years to a parent's education, the data indicate. Beyond the economic effects, of course, marriage has a wide variety of other benefits for adults and children.

Access to Birth Control

Unfortunately, we rarely teach the importance of marriage to young men and women in low-income communities. For decades now, the schools, the welfare and health care system, public authorities, and the media have refused to address this subject. They have failed so much as to tell youth that having a child outside marriage is not a good idea.

Liberals, who attribute unwed childbearing to lack of access to birth control, have attempted to address the problem by pedaling contraception. Yet research shows that low-income women who become pregnant outside marriage (whether as minors or adults) report that they almost never got that way because they lacked knowledge about, or access to, birth control.

These women say they highly value motherhood. They report that their births generally weren't unintentional—or at least not completely so.

The promise of the American Dream depends on strong marriages.

The Benefits of Marriage

Promisingly, a few states, Georgia and Kansas among them, are taking action to stem the breakdown of marriage and the increase in unwed births. Arkansas and the rest of the states can take similar steps.

A good place to start: simply telling boys and girls that it's important to wait to have a baby until after marriage. This could involve a public service campaign using billboards and online ads, or making sure Title X clinics offer educational pamphlets on the benefits of marriage.

The options are many. And the promise of the American Dream depends on strong marriages.

Kay Hymowitz, author of *Marriage and Caste in America: Separate and Unequal Families in a Post-Marital Age*, noted in a 2007 lecture at The Heritage Foundation that "erasing the bond between marriage and child rearing leads to a weakening of our country's ability to carry out . . . its promise of fairness, equality, opportunity and prosperity."

Hymowitz added: "Instead, the result is separate and unequal families as far as the eye can see."

It's long since time for Arkansas, and every other state in the union, to address the growing inequality created by the rapid rise in childbearing outside marriage.

Marriage Is Not the Solution to Ending Poverty

Joy Moses

Joy Moses is a senior policy analyst with the Poverty and Prosperity program at the Center for American Progress.

Last week [September 13, 2012] the U.S. Census Bureau released new data on poverty in America—the verdict being that the numbers reflecting 15 percent of Americans living in poverty, while still unacceptably high, have stabilized after successive years of recession-related increases. Unfortunately, the release of the new numbers hasn't been accompanied with a renewed and expansive national discussion about constructive ways of making serious progress in solving the nation's poverty problem. Some conservatives (like those with the Heritage Foundation) continue to offer up overly simplistic solutions—mainly that more women need to get married. But putting the spotlight on marriage as a silver-bullet solution to poverty takes us in the wrong direction by placing the focus on a symptom rather than the larger disease of economic insecurity (or a lack of good jobs and wages).

Three Approaches to Solving Poverty

There are significant reasons for focusing on jobs versus marriage in trying to solve poverty (even as marriage concerns are given the proper respect they deserve). Here are several approaches to take in addressing the problem of poverty:

- *Pursue common-sense options.* What is more reasonable: saying to a single mother, "We have created a job opportunity that is stable and pays well"—a job that allows her to provide for herself and her family; or saying to that same single mother, "You should just get married," and then wait for her to find a partner (if she doesn't already have one), hope he proposes, and hope the groom is not also having problems finding a stable, well-paying job? Not only is the first option a more direct route to the goal of lifting this single mother and her family out of poverty, but it also involves less hoping and more doing.

- *Recognize that full-time, year-round work matters.* Conservative marriage proponents accurately point out that single-mother families have higher poverty than married-couple families. Yet there is another important differential: The single-mother poverty rate of 40.9 percent dramatically drops to 13.4 percent for those single-mother families where the mother has full-time, year-round employment, suggesting the tremendous value of stable work for single mothers. In fact, this did help stabilize this year's poverty numbers. Although real earnings dropped compared to last year, 2.2 million people (including 206,000 single mothers) moved into full-time, year-round work. Access to work supports such as stable and secure child care help women reach this goal of full-time, year-round employment.

- *Acknowledge that men have their own challenges.* Some advocating the marriage solution fail to acknowledge the challenges facing low-income men that limit their ability to provide for a family or be viewed as desirable marriage partners. Men with limited education have experienced declining employment rates and wages over the last couple decades. For the subset of single mothers already attached to a partner, the economic benefits of marriage may not be overwhelmingly clear. According to 2011 Census data on families with children, 27 percent of male live-in partners were not working, although most were looking for work. A significant number, 39 percent, earned less than $15,000 a year. These daunting numbers not only reflect the challenges tied to the recession and the ongoing period of recovery but they also point to the employment challenges of men with limited education. Most men who are live-in partners, 67 percent, have a high school diploma or less and typically have higher rates of unemployment than men who choose to marry.

Marriage as a Solution to Poverty

In short, considering marriage as a silver-bullet solution to poverty is simply not a sensible approach. It relies too heavily on the presumption that a partner will always be available and that all marriages will last until dependent children are grown. Also, when it comes to low-income couples, there is a higher degree of probability that male partners are struggling with employment and income issues that make it difficult for them to provide for their families. And finally, policymakers could go a long way toward achieving the poverty-reduction goal by simply taking the more direct route of helping more women and men secure full-time, year-round employment.

Despite these factors, marriage remains critically important and worthy of attention—not as a remedy but as a symptom of a much larger problem: the economic insecurity of those at the bottom of the economic ladder. Declines in well-paying jobs, unemployment, growing income inequality, and persistent poverty influence couples not to marry while generating pressures and conflict on those who are married, leading to separations and divorce. It is indeed worthwhile to monitor and provide meaningful aid for this extraordinarily important symptom—the weakening and dividing of families—but to ultimately cure poverty, the nation must meaningfully address the problem of economic insecurity. Good job opportunities and quality wages will make young adults marriage ready, life ready, and increase their chances of success for the long haul.

CHAPTER 4

What Strategies Would Benefit the Homeless in America?

Chapter Preface

According to the US Department of Housing and Urban Development's 2011 Annual Homeless Assessment Report (AHAR), an estimated 1,502,196 people used an emergency shelter or transitional housing program during 2011. On any given night in January 2011, 636,017 people were homeless and 107,148 of those were chronically homeless. Homelessness in the United States costs taxpayers millions of dollars through emergency shelters, hospitalization and medical care, police intervention, incarceration, and other services. There is widespread debate about the best way to address homelessness, but what is not in dispute is that homelessness is a costly social problem.

According to a 2010 study by the US Department of Housing and Urban Development (HUD), "The emergency shelter system may be an 'adequate' response to an immediate housing crisis for most individuals, but is an expensive solution to family homelessness."[1] According to HUD, the average costs for first-time homelessness for individuals ranged from $1,634 to $2,308, whereas for families, average cost per household ranged from $3,184 to $20,031. Thus, addressing the housing needs of the homeless in the most cost-effective manner is a pressing issue for federal, state, and local governments.

The homeless population disproportionately uses emergency departments of hospitals for medical care, in part due to the fact that most lack health insurance. Legally, hospital emergency departments must serve everybody regardless of their ability to pay. According to a report in the *New England Journal of Medicine*, when homeless people do enter the hospital, they spend an average of four days longer per visit than

---

1. Brooke Spellman et al., "Costs Associated with First-Time Homelessness for Families and Individuals," US Department of Housing and Urban Development, March 2010. http://www.huduser.org/publications/pdf/Costs_Homeless.pdf.

non-homeless people, resulting in extra costs. Addressing the healthcare needs of the homeless in a manner that reduces costly emergency department visits is a pressing issue for communities.

Homelessness also proves costly with respect to law enforcement and imprisonment. Laws vary from city to city, but many common behaviors of homeless people are themselves illegal, including sleeping in public parks or in cars, sitting or sleeping on sidewalks, soliciting for money on public streets, and urinating or defecating in public. Law enforcement is called upon to enforce these laws, which can result in jail or prison time. According to research by the Vera Institute of Justice, the average cost of one year in state prison in fiscal year 2010 was $31,286. Laws that criminalize activities associated with being homeless, coupled with the high cost of imprisonment, make homelessness a drain on law enforcement resources.

The Substance Abuse and Mental Health Services Administration (SAMHSA) reports that approximately 30 percent of people who are chronically homeless have mental health conditions and 50 percent also have substance abuse problems. Failing to treat the high rate of mental health problems and substance abuse problems among the homeless is costly since it ends up driving up emergency room visits and increasing law enforcement intervention.

There are a variety of proposed solutions for addressing homelessness. In an era of dwindling state budgets, the economic costs of the homeless are of particular concern. In the debate about how to address the problem of homelessness, costs are bound to be an important factor.

Investment in Affordable Housing Is the Best Way to End Homelessness

Mary Cunningham

Mary Cunningham is a senior research associate in the Metropolitan Housing and Communities Center at the Urban Institute.

The housing crisis and corresponding recession will hit the poorest Americans the hardest. Many families and the most vulnerable citizens—those growing older, those living with disabilities, low-income children, and youth—will fall through the cracks into homelessness. As they struggle to get by, the systems set up to help them are strained beyond measure: state and local budgets are reporting large deficits; foundations are watching their endowments and the stock market; nonprofits are feeling the squeeze as donors tighten their belts; and the federal government is spending taxpayer dollars on bank bailouts and the ongoing wars in Iraq and Afghanistan, leaving little for investing in housing programs. Until recently, some communities were making progress—or at least holding the line—on ending homelessness. Today, the grim economic forecast, along with an across-the-board budget crunch, bodes poorly for these communities and the people they serve.

A Halt in Progress

In 2000, the National Alliance to End Homelessness developed a plan to end homelessness in the United States within 10 years. This plan inspired communities to employ new, research-driven and -supported approaches, including permanent supportive housing and rapid rehousing programs. These strategies, hailed as a significant "paradigm shift" in how communities respond to homelessness, were showing progress—until recently. Today, the economic crisis is making it difficult for communities to keep up with the increased demand for homeless services. Cities across the nation that were once reporting declines in homelessness are reporting increases and requests for emergency assistance, particularly among families.

It has been nearly 10 years since communities embarked on efforts to end homelessness. Today, there are numerous accomplishments to acknowledge, challenges to endure, and new setbacks to overcome. This brief examines the current state of homelessness in America, how community responses are changing, what is working, and, most important, what policymakers should be doing to move forward, not backward....

Today, over 200 plans to end homelessness are in place across the country, and hundreds more are under development.

The Movement to End Homelessness

During the 1980s and 1990s when widespread homelessness emerged, the response came largely in the form of emergency shelter and transitional housing. At the time, most policymakers and advocates thought homelessness was a temporary problem—a result of the recession, the crack epidemic, and the deinstitutionalization of people with mental disabilities. Over time, largely because of a significant loss in affordable housing during the same period, homelessness became a permanent fixture in American society. Today, HUD [US Department of Housing and Urban Development] funds approximately 422,000 emergency shelter and transitional housing beds, and the federal government spends $2.4 billion annually on homeless services programs.

Despite the significant buildup of emergency and transitional housing, homelessness has remained a problem, leaving many communities frustrated and hopeless. While emergency services are critical to meeting the immediate needs of homeless people, they do not provide people with what they need the most—permanent housing. Because of this, shelter-based responses have often been described as "managing the problem" rather than ending it. Further, while transitional housing's primary goal is improving economic self-sufficiency through employment so individuals and families can live independently after some time, its success rates are mixed. Sixteen percent who leave transitional housing remain homeless, 35 percent continue to rely on housing subsidies, and only 28 percent move to permanent housing without a housing subsidy. Even those who successfully overcome personal challenges find themselves ill equipped to afford housing in today's tight rental markets. These findings raise questions about which households should be targeted for transitional housing and whether it would be more cost-effective to provide households with a housing voucher sooner rather than later.

Frustrated by the lack of progress, in 2000, the National Alliance to End Homelessness announced a plan to end homelessness in 10 years. The core of the plan was helping people get back into permanent housing; it called on communities to transform their homeless systems, ensure rapid rehousing, and emphasize targeting interventions based on the needs of individuals and families, with the deepest housing subsidies and most intensive services going to those with the highest needs. The plan also called for significantly increasing the availability of affordable housing and the strength of the social safety net. In 2001, a few communities—Chicago [Illinois], Indianapolis [Indiana], and Memphis [Tennessee]—heeded the call to action and announced the first community plans to end homelessness.

Not long after, President [George W.] Bush announced an initiative to end chronic homelessness among disabled adults who were homeless repeatedly or for long periods, and the newly invigorated Interagency Council on Homelessness and HUD began encouraging communities to develop plans to end homelessness. Congress committed to creating 150,000 permanent supportive housing units. The national leadership led to hundreds of community planners across the country— mayors, governors, nonprofits, the private sector, and advocates—joining forces to end homelessness among individuals, families, and youth in their city or state. Today, over 200 plans to end homelessness are in place across the country, and hundreds more are under development. Taken together, these efforts represent a national movement to end homelessness. While some plans remain on the shelf, many communities are implementing their blueprints. This work is producing tangible results and has, in many cities, changed how communities respond to homelessness.

The Notion of Housing Readiness

A majority of the plans call for shifting to Housing First approaches that help people who experience long-term homelessness access housing rapidly, and then, after the household is stably housed, provide services to help with housing and economic stability. This approach challenges the popularly held notion of "housing readiness"—that people who experience homelessness must overcome their personal challenges, such as mental illness, substance abuse, and chronic health conditions, before entering housing. The core of this belief is that many of these problems are what led homeless people to homelessness in the first place; therefore, to end their homelessness, programs have to end the personal problems. The empirical evidence, however, shows that this is not true.

The impetus for the shift from housing readiness programs to Housing First programs is due, in part, to research from the University of Pennsylvania. It shows a small subset (about 10 percent) of the single adult homeless population is using 50 percent of the shelter services available, and that deploying Housing First and permanent supportive housing can help chronically homeless people with serious mental illness, including substance use disorders, access and maintain housing. Importantly, the data show that the cost of permanent supportive housing is offset by savings in public services (such as emergency room visits, jail stays, and mental health facilities) that homeless people use while living on the street or in a shelter. In other words, it costs a lot to do nothing about homelessness.

Other studies show similar findings: one randomly controlled study of Pathways to Housing, the program credited as one of the first Housing First models for chronically homeless adults, showed that the treatment group (those who received permanent supportive housing under a Housing First umbrella) reported spending less time homeless and more time stably housed than the control group. A study of two San Francisco [California] permanent supportive housing sites found that 81 percent of residents remained in housing for at least one year, and that housing placement reduced emergency department and inpatient services. Together, this research debunks the notion of "housing readiness."

Permanent Supportive Housing Programs

A body of research on how to respond to family homelessness has also emerged. Most families who experience homelessness have different needs than chronically homeless adults. They have lower rates of substance abuse and mental health challenges than homeless adults, and homeless families' characteristics more closely match other low-income families'. For these reasons, helping homeless families get back into housing largely depends on their ability to pay rent and their capacity to navigate the rental market, as well as the availability of affordable housing in the community. Housing vouchers alone can help families exit homelessness. The problem is that there are not enough vouchers for every family who needs one; further, not every family that experiences homelessness needs a voucher.

The data show that declines in homelessness correspond with significant increases in permanent supportive housing.

Some researchers argue that most families can exit homelessness with relatively little assistance—enough for the first month's rent and security deposit, for example. This theory is largely untested, though shallow housing subsidies ($175–$475 a month, depending on household size) can prevent homelessness among people living with HIV/AIDS. Program data from Hennepin County, Minnesota's rapid rehousing program—one of the first in the country—support the argument that many families, those with the lowest barriers to housing, can be rapidly rehoused with a one-time infusion of cash assistance and transitional services, while those with the highest barriers to housing are targeted for permanent supportive housing. The big policy question is how to assess and target different levels of housing subsidies and services to appropriately match family needs. Congress recently appropriated $25 million for a rapid rehousing demonstration that will allow communities to test this question empirically.

These changes in practice are producing results. A handful of communities—San Francisco, California; Portland, Oregon; New York City, New York; Denver, Colorado; and Norfolk, Virginia—were implementing Housing First initiatives and showing declines in homelessness and increases in permanent housing for homeless people. In 2007, HUD was able to measure change in homelessness from year to year for the first time ever nationally, using one-night point-in-time counts collected by CoCs [Continuums of Care] from across the country. Using these data, HUD reported a national decline of 11 percent in homelessness from 2006 to 2007 and a 30 percent decrease in the number of chronically homeless adults from 2005 to 2007. While these data have some limitations—the study's authors attributed this decline to both real progress in helping homeless individuals and families get back into housing and changes in data collection methods—HUD and many advocates, researchers, and homeless service providers celebrated these findings as a sign that Housing First efforts and targeted permanent supportive housing programs were working.

Certainly the data show that declines in homelessness correspond with significant increases in permanent supportive housing. From 2002 to 2007, 65,000 and 72,000 units were created; about half were already open in 2007, and the remainder were still under development. When completed, these units will effectively double the stock of permanent supportive housing. According to the Corporation for Supportive Housing, about 20 percent of the permanent supportive housing beds created during that period went to families; 47 percent went to chronically homeless adults, and 33 percent went to other vulnerable single adults. Today there are 188,000 permanent supportive housing beds across the country. . . .

Policymakers have a choice: they can continue to pour resources into short-term fixes . . . or they can focus on long-term solutions.

The Need to Invest in Housing

Today many communities are holding on tightly to any progress in ending homelessness. Economic problems, the foreclosure crisis, broader factors, and the strain on emergency response systems for poor people could lead to significant, across-the-board increases in homelessness and will likely result in the need for more emergency shelter. But, as history shows, the answer is not building more temporary shelter—it is increasing the availability of affordable housing. Policymakers face a daunting to do list with competing priorities; decisions will be difficult. They should focus on the lessons learned from research during the past decade and continue the effort to end homelessness by investing in housing, specifically:

- *Bring Housing First and permanent supportive housing to scale.* While communities have adopted and implemented Housing First programs, the innovations remain small-scale. To ensure continued progress on ending homelessness among adults with long homeless histories, Congress should expand efforts to create permanent supportive housing. The Corporation for Supportive Housing and the National Alliance to End Homelessness estimate that 90,000 units are needed to end chronic homelessness among single adults. These units should be targeted to those with the highest needs, including older, chronically homeless people with significant health problems. In addition, Congress should significantly expand access to permanent supportive housing for families that need it. This means targeting these higher-service intensity interventions to families with severe substance abuse and mental health problems. Finally, the homelessness problem in New Orleans [Louisiana] can no longer be ignored. Congress must provide enough permanent supportive housing units for people with serious mental illness and physical health problems and additional resources for housing subsidies to the working poor who cannot afford the high cost of rental housing after Hurricane Katrina [hit in 2005].

- *Expand rapid rehousing for families.* To better serve families, homeless systems must shift their resources

159

from costly transitional housing programs toward rapid rehousing programs that provide different housing subsidy and service levels to families based on their needs (i.e., shelter diversion assistance and shallow and short-term housing subsidies with transitional services and permanent supportive housing). To do this, Congress must appropriate additional resources to rapid rehousing programs and give communities the flexibility to convert transitional housing resources to either short-term interim housing or permanent supportive housing for high-need families. Once families are living in stable, safe, affordable housing, providers should connect them to community-based supports to help them maintain housing stability and improve their economic well-being.

- *Fully invest in rental housing and homelessness programs for veterans.* No one who served in the United States military should be homeless. To help veterans who are already homeless, Congress should invest in the HUD-VASH [HUD-Veterans Affairs Supportive Housing] program, fully funding 66,000 HUD-VASH vouchers for chronically homeless veterans. In addition, GAO [Government Accountability Office] data indicate that many veterans are severely rent burdened and have trouble accessing HUD housing programs. This demonstrates the need for a rental assistance program for veterans. It could come in the form of a housing supplement to VA [US Department of Veterans Affairs] benefits. Further, to prevent homelessness among new veterans, Congress should invest in a pilot homelessness prevention program.

- *Make mainstream systems accountable.* During the past two decades, the homeless system has become the de facto safety net for the most vulnerable people. Mainstream systems such as prisons, jails, mental health facilities, hospitals, child welfare agencies, foster care, and juvenile justice can all help prevent homelessness by improving discharge planning to include a housing component. There should be zero tolerance for discharges into homelessness, and policymakers should provide incentives to mainstream systems to prevent shelter entry. In some communities, the Department of Corrections is partnering with homeless service providers to provide permanent supportive housing for people cycling between homelessness and incarceration; these investments can save taxpayers money and decrease recidivism. Discharge programs like these, though promising, remain small. Policymakers should expand funding to facilitate these partnerships and provide housing resources. Funding for these housing programs should not come from McKinney-Vento homeless assistance programs, which are already struggling to meet the needs of those sleeping on the street or in shelters.

- *Ramp up emergency prevention programs.* As researcher Martha Burt has observed, "homelessness is America's revolving door crisis." Indeed, the data on homeless service use show that without considerable prevention efforts, there will be a continual flow of people experiencing homelessness and residential instability. The current economic crisis will leave even more people at risk of homelessness. Building more emergency shelters is not the answer. Through an economic stimulus package, Congress should significantly increase funding for homelessness prevention. These resources should focus on helping people stay in housing and—for those who are already homeless—get back into housing by providing emergency assistance for household expenses (e.g., utility payments), short-term or medium-term rental assistance, and housing relocation and stabilization services. Further, as Congress drafts legislation to respond to the foreclosure crisis, special attention should go to renters living in properties at risk for foreclosure; these households need notice to move and relocation assistance to transition to stable housing.

- *Invest in housing programs that help build stronger people and families.* The research is clear: an adequate supply of affordable rental housing is the key ingredient to preventing widespread homelessness. To end homelessness, Congress must rebuild rental housing policies, invest in publicly assisted housing, and develop affordable housing in the private market. Cost is no excuse; it is a question of priorities. In the past, Congress has favored home ownership and has extended significant financial benefits to home owners. Much more attention should be paid to investing in rental housing by significantly increasing public investment in housing vouchers and financial incentives to state and local governments to produce affordable housing. Congress should fund an additional 200,000 vouchers a year for the next five years and significantly invest in affordable housing programs—such as 202 and 811—for the elderly and people with disabilities. Other low-cost housing, such as SROs [single room occupancy], is needed to ensure single adults with low wages can afford housing instead of relying on emergency shelter or motels. Finally, Congress should fully fund the National Housing Trust Fund at $5 billion annually.

The United States is at a critical juncture. A decade of research has shown what works in ending homelessness, and hundreds of communities were implementing these evidence-based solutions and—until recently—reporting declines in homelessness. The economic turmoil threatens this hard-earned progress, significantly increasing the number of people at risk of homelessness and, thus, the need for stable and affordable housing. Policymakers have a choice: they can continue to pour resources into short-term fixes—like emergency shelter and transitional housing—and watch the homeless numbers swell, or they can focus on long-term solutions by seriously investing in affordable housing programs. Research shows that the latter is better public policy and can be cost-effective.

Increased Funding Is Needed for Federal Low-Income Housing Programs

Douglas Rice and Barbara Sard

Douglas Rice is senior policy analyst and Barbara Sard is vice president for housing policy at the Center on Budget and Policy Priorities.

One-third of all American households are renters, as are about half of *low-income* households. Yet too many renters pay housing costs that are unaffordable. The problem has grown in recent years, according to Census data, and is especially acute among households with the lowest incomes:

- *More than 8 million renter households paid more than half of their income for rent and basic utilities in 2007,* the most recent year for which data are available. Under federal standards, housing costs are considered unaffordable if they exceed 30 percent of household income.

- *Nearly all of these households had low incomes* (i.e., at or below 80 percent of their state's median income). Two out of three of them had extremely low incomes (i.e., below 30 percent of the state median income, a level that is roughly equivalent to the federal poverty line).

- *The number of low-income renter households that paid more than half of their income for housing increased by 2 million, or 32 percent, between 2000 and 2007.*

- *Many of these households are working households.* Excluding those headed by people who are elderly or have disabilities, low-income households that pay more than half of their income for housing report that members worked a combined average of 25 hours per week for 25 weeks during the prior year.

Since 1995, federal spending on low-income housing assistance has fallen by well over 20 percent.

The High Cost of Rental Housing

When housing costs are too high, the impact on low-income renters can be severe and enduring. Families can be forced to cut back on food, clothing, medications, or transportation. High housing costs also can compel families to live in housing that is overcrowded or unhealthy, or in neighborhoods with failing schools, high rates of crime, or limited access to basic services. Moreover, research suggests that housing instability and homelessness can hinder the healthy development of children in ways that have a lasting impact.

This problem is likely to get worse. Over the past decade, the number of renter households has grown faster than the supply of rental housing, and there is little reason to expect this trend to change in the near future. Although rents may decline in some communities as a result of the foreclosure crisis and recession, wages will fall as well and unemployment is already rising.

Yet despite rental housing's importance to the well-being of a large share of American households—and the clear failure of the private market to meet the existing need—it has been the neglected step-child of federal housing policy. Since 1995, federal spending on low-income housing assistance has fallen *by well over 20 percent* both as a share of all non-defense discretionary spending and as a share of the Gross Domestic

Product (GDP). Even when combined with the Low-Income Housing Tax Credit, the federal government's total commitment to low-income housing assistance is less than one-third the size of the three largest tax breaks provided to homeowners (such as the home mortgage interest deduction).

A Weakening of Federal Low-Income Housing Programs

The fiscal pressure on low-income housing programs increased considerably during the [George W.] Bush Administration. The Administration's annual budgets gave priority to deep tax cuts and increases in defense and homeland security funding. When sizeable deficits emerged in 2003 and 2004, the Administration and Congress turned primarily to reductions in domestic discretionary (i.e., non-entitlement) programs. Discretionary funding for federal low-income housing programs, for example, was slashed in 2005; after rising modestly in 2006 and 2007, it fell again in 2008. In 2008, total funding for all low-income housing programs was $2.0 billion (5.0 percent) below the 2004 level, adjusted for inflation. For some programs, such as public housing, these cuts came on top of earlier funding reductions.

These reductions in funding, combined in some cases with policy changes that exacerbated funding instability, have weakened the three major federal low-income housing programs at a time when the need for assistance is rising sharply:

- *Housing Choice Vouchers.* This program provides about 2 million low-income families with vouchers to help pay for housing that they find in the private market. More than half of these families include children; another third include seniors or people with disabilities. Between 2004 and 2006, voucher assistance for approximately 150,000 low-income families was eliminated as funding shortfalls compelled housing agencies to serve fewer families. Many agencies also cut costs in other ways that have discouraged landlords from renting units to families with vouchers and limited the ability of families to use vouchers to move to neighborhoods with lower crime rates and better schools.

- *Public Housing.* The nation's 14,000 public housing developments, located in more than 3,500 communities, provide affordable homes to nearly 1.2 million families, nearly two-thirds of which include seniors or people with disabilities. In recent years, deep and persistent funding shortfalls have forced housing agencies to take steps such as increasing costs for low-income tenants, delaying repairs, and cutting back on security. Also, an increasing number of agencies appear to have concluded that they can no longer sustain all of their developments and are seeking to remove them from the program. Some 165,000 units of public housing have been lost since 1995 and not replaced; these losses are likely to continue.

Two million new vouchers . . . would help roughly 3 million low-income households over the 10-year period to secure decent, affordable homes.

- *Section 8 Project-Based Rental Assistance.* This program is a public-private partnership in which private owners sign contracts with HUD [US Department of Housing and Urban Development] to provide affordable homes to nearly 1.3 million low-income families, three-quarters of which are headed by people who are elderly or have disabilities. Over the past few years, a series of changes in HUD funding policies—designed in part to save money—caused widespread and lengthy delays in payments to owners and have undermined confidence in this program. Some 10,000 to 15,000 units of affordable Section 8 housing are lost every year as owners exit the program; these losses are likely to accelerate if HUD fails to restore owner confidence. At greatest risk are approximately 150,000 units whose owners already have strong financial incentives to leave the program because the rents they receive are well below market rates.

Only one in four low-income households eligible for federal housing assistance receives it because of funding limitations. Unless the new Administration and Congress set a different course, an even smaller proportion of the low-income households is likely to be assisted in the future, further widening the gap between housing needs and available federal assistance.

The Need for New Resources

Following nearly a decade of neglect—and the bursting of the housing bubble, which has exposed the limitations of an unbalanced emphasis on homeownership—it is time for the new Administration and Congress to revitalize federal rental housing policy. Policymakers need to develop a comprehensive strategy to address the private market's failure to provide sufficient affordable housing. But in the meantime, they should pursue the following goals, which should form part of any viable comprehensive strategy:

- *Preserve existing public and private assisted housing,* in its current location or in other locations that will better serve families. Specifically, the Administration and Congress should commit the necessary resources to:

   Restore full operating funding for public housing;

   Address the substantial backlog of capital repairs in public housing;

   Re-establish reliable renewal funding for project-based Section 8 contracts;

Provide incentives and assistance to encourage private owners to renew their participation in the Section 8 project-based rental assistance program; and

Improve energy efficiency in public and private assisted housing.

- *Fully utilize the housing vouchers Congress has already authorized.* Enacting the funding provisions of the Section 8 Voucher Reform Act (SEVRA), which the House passed in 2007, would encourage housing agencies to use voucher funds more efficiently. As a result, significantly more low-income families would receive voucher assistance. No additional funding would be required in the first year these vouchers were used.

- *Expand assistance to help more families* secure stable, affordable housing in safe neighborhoods with access to good schools, steady jobs, and other essential services they need to improve their lives. The most flexible, cost-effective way to do this is to fund new, "incremental" housing vouchers. Two million new vouchers (for example, funding 200,000 new vouchers per year over ten years), would help roughly 3 million low-income households over the 10-year period to secure decent, affordable homes; lift an estimated 3.3 million people, including 1.6 million children, out of poverty; and prevent 230,000 people, including 110,000 children, from becoming homeless. New vouchers could also be used to promote other policy goals, such as the development of affordable housing near mass transit (to reduce energy use and promote climate change goals) or as part of a broad strategy to expand educational and economic opportunities for low-income families.

To expand housing voucher assistance to 2 million new families would require a substantial investment: roughly $8,000 for each voucher in the first year, plus the cost of renewal of each voucher in subsequent years. This investment would pay considerable dividends, however, in terms of reduced poverty and homelessness and better opportunities for families struggling to improve their lives while making ends meet.

The Solution to Chronic Homelessness Is Permanent Supportive Housing

National Alliance to End Homelessness

The National Alliance to End Homelessness is a nonprofit, non-partisan organization committed to preventing and ending homelessness in the United States.

Nearly 10 years ago, the federal government made a commitment to end chronic homelessness. Since then, a great deal of progress has been made on that goal, much of it due to incentives and directives from the federal government, and much of it due to the benefits of reducing chronic homelessness. This brief will examine:

- Who experiences chronic homelessness;

- The progress made in reducing chronic homelessness;

- Federal policies and local practices that contributed to that progress; and

- What policymakers can do to finish the job of ending chronic homelessness in the United States.

The Problem of Chronic Homelessness

Each year, an estimated 1.6 million people access homeless shelter services, though many more people experience homelessness and sleep on the streets, obtain assistance through a domestic violence shelter, or are otherwise not counted. Though most spend only a short period of time homeless, a small group of people experiences chronic homelessness. This

National Alliance to End Homelessness, "Chronic Homelessness: Policy Solutions," *Chronic Homelessness Brief*, March 2010, pp. 1–4. Copyright © 2010 by National Alliance to End Homelessness. All rights reserved. Republished with permission.

small group may spend months or even years homeless or cy-cling in and out of homelessness and other institutional care. Chronic homelessness is extremely costly to publicly funded systems of care, costing tens of thousands of dollars annually for each chronically homeless individual.

Research and experience over the past 20 years has shown that there is a cost-effective solution to chronic homelessness known as permanent supportive housing. Communities across the country that have instituted that approach have reported a decline in the number of people living on the streets and in shelters. Chronic homelessness is a problem with a known so-lution, and federal leadership on implementing that solution has resulted in tangible reductions of this tragedy and can continue to do so.

Despite the severity of the problem, communities across the country have been making progress at reducing home-lessness.

Chronically homeless people have disabilities such as seri-ous mental illness, chronic substance use disorders, or chronic medical issues and are homeless repeatedly or for long periods of time. They often cycle in and out of homeless shelters, jails, hospitals, and treatment programs. Because of the high service needs of this group, they use a disproportionate share of shel-ter beds and other public resources. A landmark study of single adult shelters found that chronically homeless individu-als account for approximately 10 percent of shelter users, but consume about 50 percent of shelter resources. This research led to federal initiatives focused on chronically homeless indi-viduals unaccompanied by children. However, recently enacted legislation revised the federal definition of chronic homeless-ness to include families with children.

People experiencing chronic homelessness have the following characteristics:

- Typically male (79–86 percent), and middle aged (60 percent are between 35 and 54)

- Usually live on the streets or in places not meant for human habitation (63 percent unsheltered)

- Near universal presence of disabilities (frequently multiple disabilities at once)

- Frequent use of emergency rooms, hospitals, mental health services, veterans' services, substance abuse detoxification and treatment, and criminal justice resources

The most recent available data shows that there are approximately 124,000 chronically homeless individuals in the United States, accounting for about 20 percent of the overall homeless population. There is not enough data to estimate precisely how many families are chronically homeless, however, evidence suggests approximately 10,000 to 15,000. Despite the severity of the problem, communities across the country have been making progress at reducing homelessness. Between 2005 and 2008, chronic homelessness fell nationally by 28 percent. Some communities have witnessed even steeper declines:

- Quincy, MA witnessed a 50 percent reduction in chronic homelessness between 2005 and 2009.

- Chronic homelessness in Norfolk, VA fell by almost 40 percent between 2006 and 2008.

- There was a 36 percent decline in chronic homelessness in Denver, CO between 2005 and 2007.

- Portland, OR found that the number of chronically homelessness people sleeping outside fell 70 percent between 2005 and 2007.

- Chronic homelessness in Portland, ME declined by 49 percent between 2004 and 2007.

- Wichita, KS reduced chronic homelessness 61 percent between 2005 and 2009.

Strategies to Reduce Chronic Homelessness

Reductions in chronic homelessness are largely the result of coordinated and focused efforts by communities to provide permanent supportive housing for chronically homeless individuals. Beginning in 2002, communities began developing and implementing Ten Year Plans to End Homelessness, which generally included strategies for addressing chronic homelessness. To date, more than 270 communities have completed Ten Year Plans. Much of this activity is a response to federal incentives to focus attention and resources on chronic homelessness. Communities are also making progress preventing chronic homelessness by intervening when homeless people are in hospitals, correctional facilities, or in other institutional care facilities.

Permanent Supportive Housing. The most successful intervention for ending chronic homelessness is permanent supportive housing, which couples permanent housing with supportive services that target the specific needs of an individual or family. Housing is most often provided in the form of a rental subsidy, such as a Section 8 Housing Choice Voucher or a subsidy through the McKinney-Vento Homeless Assistance program. Permanent supportive housing units can be located in a single building ("single site") or be scattered across a number of locations ("scattered-site"). The most effective approach to permanent supportive housing is Housing First, meaning that tenants are placed into housing before attempting to resolve their services needs, rather than after.

Because of their high level of mental health, substance abuse, and physical needs, chronically homeless individuals and families generally need ongoing supportive services. Services provided through permanent supportive housing can include health care, substance abuse treatment, mental health treatment, employment counseling, connections with mainstream benefits like Medicaid, and countless others.

Research has shown that coupling these services with permanent housing is highly effective at maintaining housing stability, but also helps improve health outcomes and decreases the use of publicly-funded institutions. Below is a sample of research findings on the effects of permanent supportive housing:

- A study of homeless people in New York City with serious mental illness found that providing permanent supportive housing to the individuals directly resulted in a 60 percent decrease in emergency shelter use for clients, as well as decreases in the use of public medical and mental health services and city jails and state prisons.

- A 2009 Seattle [Washington] study found that moving chronic inebriates into permanent supportive housing resulted in an approximately 33 percent decline in alcohol use for clients.

- Research on the overall costs to the taxpayer of permanent supportive housing has consistently found the costs to the taxpayers to be about the same or lower than having a chronically homeless individual sleep in an emergency shelter.

Prevention. Another way that communities have reduced chronic homelessness is through prevention. Because so many chronically homeless people cycle in and out of jails, prisons, hospitals, psychiatric facilities, and treatment programs, some of the individuals most vulnerable to becoming chronically homeless can be identified in advance. For example, in Quincy, MA, of all clients going to homeless service providers, 49 percent had previous involvement with the Department of Mental Health and 22 percent had been involved with social services previously. Using this information, Quincy changed the discharge policies in its systems of care, which contributed to a 50 percent reduction in chronic homelessness between 2005 and 2009. These systems should also address the housing needs of their clients more generally, ensuring that, for example, people receiving outpatient mental health services are screened for housing stability and provided with housing assistance if appropriate.

Despite the successes of the past several years and how much we know about what does work—permanent supportive housing, prevention, and targeting—challenges to ending chronic homelessness remain.

Targeting. Permanent supportive housing and prevention have proven most effective in the places where they have been targeted to people with the most extensive service needs. For example, Seattle, WA's 1811 Eastlake Apartments provide housing to homeless people with the most extensive health problems. As a result, the program saves nearly $30,000 per tenant per year in publicly funded services, all while achieving better housing and health outcomes.

Among families with children, the most promising targeting strategies focus on families who are repeatedly homeless. About 75 percent of families that enter shelter are able to quickly exit with little or no assistance and never return. Another about 20 percent of families have longer stays in shelter but are able to access and remain in permanent housing. The remaining families are repeatedly homeless and should be prioritized for permanent supportive housing.

Despite the successes of the past several years and how much we know about what does work—permanent supportive housing, prevention, and targeting—challenges to ending chronic homelessness remain. Most importantly, more permanent supportive housing is needed. Improving targeting and prevention in federal programs is also necessary.

With increased resources from Congress for supportive housing, we truly can end the tragedy of chronic homelessness in the United States once and for all.

In the early 2000s, the bipartisan Millennial Housing Commission and the President's New Freedom Commission on Mental Health estimated that approximately 150,000 new units of permanent supportive housing were needed to end chronic homelessness. Since then, approximately 60,000 units have been created through HUD's [US Department of Housing and Urban Development's] McKinney-Vento Homeless Assistance Grants, leaving another 90,000 still to be created. Several federal policies are needed to help create these units.

- *Increase funding for HUD's homeless assistance programs*: The most successful resource for creating permanent supportive housing has been HUD's McKinney-Vento Homeless Assistance programs, creating 5,000–10,000 units per year.

- *Coordinate housing and services*: One of the biggest challenges to creating more permanent supportive housing is the lack of coordination between federal housing and services programs. Typically providers must cobble together funding from dozens of federal and local sources, none of which are designed to work in an integrated fashion. The federal government should streamline and coordinate existing programs to facilitate the development of permanent supportive housing.

- *Lower barriers to subsidized housing programs*: Currently, barriers such as unit inspection and documentation requirements, as well as locally-imposed restrictions, make it difficult for people experiencing chronic homelessness to enter HUD subsidized housing. Congress and HUD should reduce these barriers for homeless people.

- *Improve Medicaid*: Most people experiencing chronic homelessness eventually qualify for Medicaid, but the process for determining eligibility can take several months or even years, and the services that can be reimbursed by Medicaid are limited. States should be given authority to create cost effective services coordinated with permanent supportive housing for people experiencing chronic homelessness.

- *Create simple renewable SAMHSA funding for services in permanent supportive housing*: People experiencing chronic homelessness typically have co-occurring mental health and substance use disorders. The Substance Abuse and Mental Health Services Administration (SAMHSA) has several small programs that address these needs, however they are temporary and small. SAMHSA should be a major source of renewable funding for services in supportive housing.

- *Improve services for veterans*: A large share of people who experience chronic homelessness are veterans. Congress should continue to provide funding for HUD-VASH [HUD-Veterans Affairs Supportive Housing], a successful housing and services partnership between HUD and VA [US Department of Veterans Affairs]. It should also give VA more responsibility for addressing the housing needs of veterans.

An estimated 120,000 people currently experience chronic homelessness, living in shelters, on the streets, and in other places not meant for human habitation. Luckily, years of research and practice have shown us what works to prevent and end homelessness for this group of people. Across the county, communities have begun to not only reduce chronic homelessness by using these interventions, but also to save money in the process. With increased resources from Congress for supportive housing, we truly can end the tragedy of chronic homelessness in the United States once and for all.

Solutions/Bandow: Handling America's Homeless Families

Doug Bandow

Doug Bandow is a senior fellow at the Cato Institute, a former special assistant to Presifdent Reagan, and author of Beyond Good Intentions: A Biblical View of Politics *and* The Politics of Envy: Statism as Theology.

With the economy in apparent freefall, human needs, including homelessness, have grown. Our starting point should be moral, not political.

During the dramatic biblical parable of the sheep and goats, Jesus asserts our moral responsibility rather than debates our policy approach.

Matthew quotes Jesus as telling the sheep: "For I was hungry and you gave me something to eat, I was thirsty and you gave me something to drink, I was a stranger and you invited me in." They ministered to Jesus by doing these things "for one of the least of these brothers of mine."

This duty cannot be subcontracted to government. The Bible demonstrates concentric rings of responsibility moving outward, starting with individuals who are enjoined to take care of themselves, rather than living off of others. Those who fail to care for their families are worse than unbelievers, Paul warns. The early church transferred money within and among faith communities. Finally, Paul says in Galatians, "let us do good to all people."

If the political authorities are to act, it should be because other institutions have failed to meet people's basic needs. Today, far more private than public programs serve the home-

Doug Bandow, "Handling America's Homeless Families," *The Washington Times*, May 17, 2009. Copyright © 2009 by The Washington Times. All rights reserved. Republished with permission.

less. The Catholic and Protestant doctrines of subsidiarity and sphere sovereignty, respectively, recognize that government is to respect the roles of other social institutions.

Diversity of responses is particularly important in dealing with a problem as complicated as homelessness. Even the number of homeless is disputed.

The Department of Housing and Urban Development figures homelessness on any particular night (in or out of a shelter) ran 672,000 as of January 2007—down about 10 percent from 2005. There were 84,000 homeless households, down 15 percent. Chronic homelessness ran 124,000, down 30 percent.

The drop is positive, though these numbers remain far too high, and may have turned up in the current economic imbroglio.

The answer is not simply more money for more government programs, of which there are thousands nationwide. This enormous challenge can be best met by reflecting back on the biblical model.

The reasons for homelessness run the gamut. Those in poverty long have had difficulty finding affordable housing.

Dubious mortgages, declining home prices and increasing unemployment are threatening many homeowners today. The rising tide of foreclosures puts entire families at risk.

Homelessness also often reflects personal crisis, such as family breakdown, substance abuse and/or mental illness. The deinstitutionalization movement, which sought to respect the dignity of those who had been forcibly medicated and hospitalized, left some people living on the streets. Alcohol or drug use often accentuated other problems.

The answer is not simply more money for more government programs, of which there are thousands nationwide. This enormous challenge can be best met by reflecting back on the biblical model. We need to simultaneously meet current needs, which often include illness and hunger, and reduce future problems.

First, individuals and families have a moral as well as practical imperative to behave responsibly. Americans need to relearn how to resist substance abuse, curb wasteful expenditures and save money. Borrowers and lenders alike should spend money wisely.

Second, family and friends, backed by churches and other social networks, should be the first line of defense to homelessness. The need may be as simple as temporary financial aid or an empty couch. Such informal assistance can soften the impact of unexpected hardship while preserving the dignity of those in need.

The government's safety net is best maintained by states and localities rather than by Washington.

Third, private social programs are better than government initiatives in ministering to the whole person, rather than treating those in trouble as numbers and prescribing only a check or bed. Some of the neediest require proverbial "tough love"—compassion and discipline. It is important to keep people off the street and ensure that they won't face the same problem again. That often requires changes in behavior as well as circumstance.

Obviously, charities have been affected by the current economic slump. However, this provides an opportunity for advocacy by activists and preaching by religious leaders. Those concerned about the needy must remind all of us of our duty to help, especially in difficult times. Too whom much is given, much is expected, the Bible explains.

Fourth, local initiatives are most likely to be effective in meeting needs that vary dramatically by region. Unfortunately, the results of many of the federal welfare programs, including those directed at housing, ranging from rental vouchers to Section 8 to public housing, have been ugly. The government's safety net is best maintained by states and localities rather than by Washington.

Fifth, the many federal subsidy programs used to encourage homeownership—Federal Housing Administration, Community Reinvestment Act, Fannie Mae, Freddie Mac—are ground zero of today's housing crisis and should be curbed. Attempts to solve the current crisis by artificially reinflating home values risk rewarding improvident lenders and borrowers alike, delaying painful but necessary adjustments in the housing market, and creating conditions for repeat experience in the near future.

We should instead make housing less expensive. Through exclusionary zoning (including restrictions on multifamily housing and minimum-lot size and square-footage requirements) and outmoded building codes (which reflect union interests rather than safety concerns), government has limited the housing supply and increased housing costs. Palliatives like rent control only worsen the underlying problem; government should strip away barriers to affordable housing. Doing so would help reduce homelessness.

Good people in a good society take care of those in need. That includes the homeless. But just as the problem is complex, so is the solution. And we will do best if we respond first at a human rather than at a political level.

Can Goldman Sachs Help the Homeless?

Margaret Wente

Margaret Wente is a columnist for the Globe and Mail, *a national newspaper in Canada.*

A few blocks from where I work, there's a guy who lives on a sidewalk in the Financial District. That guy is incredibly expensive. For the amount we pay in social services to keep him alive, he could practically move into the Ritz. The yearly cost of caring for a homeless person with substance abuse and mental issues (that is, most of them) ranges from $55,000 up to $134,000, according to various research studies.

Everybody knows there must be a better way. Get that guy into long-term housing and give him the social supports he needs to stabilize his life, or at least to spend less of it in hospitals and jails. That's expensive too. But it's a lot cheaper than what we do now, and certainly more humane.

Even though preventive services can often save money in the long run, governments are loath to fund them. Prevention is expensive. It requires long-term investment, which is not how governments operate. The payoffs are often hard to measure and far in the future. Effective prevention programs also require co-ordinated services, innovative and even risky new approaches, and a laser-like focus on measurable results. Governments are terrible at all these things, especially the results.

All of this explains why "social finance" is suddenly so hot. The idea behind social finance—also known as "impact investing"—is to get more private money into social projects that will pay off for society, and also for investors. If the projects get results, investors will be handsomely rewarded.

In New York City, Goldman Sachs has offered to put up $9.6-million in the form of a "social impact bond," to fund a program that's designed to keep young prisoners released from Rikers Island out of jail. The rationale for helping ex-cons is the same as for housing the homeless—keeping people out of jail saves money in the long run. The program is delivered by a non-profit group. If it can cut recidivism rates by 10 per cent over four years, Goldman gets its money back. If it does better, Goldman could make a healthy profit. A similar program, launched two years ago at Britain's Peterborough prison, is producing promising early results. More people are getting help, and local crime has fallen.

In Massachusetts, the government has been using "pay for success" contracts to cut homelessness. It figures it saves $9,423 per year for every person housed, including program costs. Fresno, Calif., is trying an asthma prevention program.

The old models are finished, and we've got to start inventing new ones.

These programs have two requirements that government programs don't have. They are tied to outcomes, not outputs. And investors only get their money back if they work. Warm feelings (which are the main output of many, if not most, social programs) aren't good enough. As Massachusetts secretary of finance Jay Gonzales told the *Boston Globe*, "There's a newfound interest . . . in changing the culture of state government to focus on results." Social financing tools "can empower governments to innovate in ways they wouldn't otherwise attempt," Mayor Michael Bloomberg told *The New York Times*.

Social finance has drawn strong support from some of the world's biggest charitable foundations, as well as from U.S. President Barack Obama. Canadian advocates include Paul

Martin and other leading thinkers, as well as a new generation of social entrepreneurs who are as interested in doing good as doing well. The Harper government also wants to jump on board, and has asked for pitches from the private and charitable sectors.

As you'd expect, not everyone is crazy about letting the private sector in the door. The NDP and other left-leaning groups detect the stench of stealth privatization. They are certain that the pursuit of profit by the likes of Goldman Sachs inevitably means less money for the needy. Other skeptics point out that designing and measuring effective programs is harder than it looks—and that it will be years before we understand if, and how well, they work.

But we also face a set of hard and unpleasant facts. Many government services are demonstrably wasteful, inefficient and ineffective. And governments are out of money. The only way they will be able to maintain the social services we already have is to deliver better results at less cost. The old models are finished, and we've got to start inventing new ones.

Giving Money to Homeless Panhandlers Is Not a Solution to Homelessness

Derek Thompson

Derek Thompson is a senior editor at The Atlantic, *where he oversees business coverage for TheAtlantic.com.*

Giving money to the homeless is an economic crisis of the heart, a tug-of-war between the instinct to alleviate suffering and the knowledge that a donation might encourage, rather than relieve, the anguish of the poor.

We're all familiar with our mothers' reasons not to empty our pockets for beggars. "The best help is a shelter not a dollar," she's told us, and "They'll only use it on [something bad] anyway!"

The studies seem to back up mom, to a degree. One report from the Department of Housing and Urban Development [HUD] found that six out of ten homeless respondents admitted problems with alcohol or drugs. Given the likelihood of self-reported bias, the actual number could be even higher. Studies on homeless income find that the typical "career panhandler" who dedicates his time overwhelmingly to begging can make between $600 and $1,500 a month. But since panhandlers often have no way to save their money, they're incentivized to spend most of their day's earnings quickly. This creates a tendency to spend on short-term relief, rather than long-term needs, which can feed this dependency on alcoholic relief.

The Case for Giving

What do economists say about the instinct to help the homeless? (For these purposes, I'm ignoring the altruism factor, the idea that if giving 50 cents makes us feel good then it's an inherently justifiable donation.) Some argue that giving cash to cash-needy people is the most efficient way to spend it. Indeed, the Congressional Budget Office has stated explicitly that the most efficient government stimulus targets the poorest Americans. And who's more indigent than a panhandler? What's more, if you donate to a charity, there are administrative costs and time-lags. If you put your money in the hands of a beggar, however, it's fast, easy, and guaranteed to be spent immediately.

But the fact that beggars are likely to spend their money quickly is also the problem. Food stamps are considered highly effective government spending, but they're earmarked for food. Unemployment benefits can go a long way, but recipients have to prove that they're looking for work. A dollar from your hand to a homeless person's carries no such strings attached.

But what would happen if we provided both money *and* strings? *Good* magazine found a British non-profit that identified 15 long-term homeless people ("rough sleepers," as they're known across the pond), asked what they needed to change their lives, and just bought it for them. Some asked for items as simple as shoes, or cash to repay a loan. One asked for a camper van. Another wanted a TV to make his hostel more livable. All were accommodated with 3,000 pounds and a "broker" to help them manage their budget. Of the 13 who agreed to take part, 11 were off the street within a year, and several entered treatment for addiction.

The upshot: *The homeless often need something more than money. They need money and direction.* For most homeless people, direction means a job and a roof. A 1999 study from HUD polled homeless people about what they needed most:

42% said help finding a job; 38% said finding housing; 30% said paying rent or utilities; 13% said training or medical care.

Both sides fail each other by being lured into fleeting sense of relief rather than a lasting solution to the structural problem of homelessness.

The Problem with Donations to Individuals

Organizations can obviously do more for the needy than we can with the change in our back pocket. But does that mean we shouldn't give, *ever?*

The consistently entertaining economist Tyler Cowen worries that giving to beggars induces bad long-term incentives. If you travel to a poor city, for example, you'll find swarms of beggars by touristy locations. If the tourists become more generous, the local beggars don't get richer, they only multiply. Generous pedestrians attract more beggars. Cowen writes:

> The more you give to beggars, the harder beggars will try. This leads to what economists call "rent exhaustion," which again limits the net gain to beggars.... If you are going to give, pick the poor person who is expecting it least.

I'm certain that there are some cases where donations to an especially needy beggar are justified. But the ultimate danger in panhandling is that we don't give to every beggar. There's not enough change in our purses. We choose to donate money based on the level of perceived need. Beggars know this, so there is an incentive on their part to exaggerate their need, by either lying about their circumstances or letting their appearance visibly deteriorate rather than seek help.

If we drop change in a beggar's hand without donating to a charity, we're acting to relieve our guilt rather than underlying crisis of poverty. The same calculus applies to the beggar who relies on panhandling for a booze hit. In short, both sides fail each other by being lured into fleeting sense of relief rather than a lasting solution to the structural problem of homelessness.

Organizations to Contact

The editors have compiled the following list of organizations concerned with the issues debated in this book. The descriptions are derived from materials provided by the organizations. All have publications or information available for interested readers. The list was compiled on the date of publication of the present volume; names, addresses, phone and fax numbers, and e-mail and Internet addresses may change. Be aware that many organizations take several weeks or longer to respond to inquiries, so allow as much time as possible.

American Enterprise Institute for Public Policy Research (AEI)
1150 17th St. NW, Washington, DC   20036
(202) 862-5800 • fax: (202) 862-7177
website: www.aei.org

The American Enterprise Institute is a private, nonpartisan, nonprofit institution committed to expanding liberty, increasing individual opportunity, and strengthening free enterprise. AEI sponsors research and education on issues of government, politics, economics, and social welfare. Among AEI's publications is the book *Prices, Poverty, and Inequality: Why Americans Are Better Off than You Think.*

Cato Institute
1000 Massachusetts Ave. NW, Washington, DC   20001-5403
(202) 842-0200 • fax: (202) 842-3490
website: www.cato.org

The Cato Institute is a public policy research foundation dedicated to the principles of individual liberty, limited government, free markets, and peace. Its scholars and analysts conduct independent, nonpartisan research on a wide range of policy issues. Among its publications are the quarterly journal of public policy analysis *Cato Journal,* the bimonthly *Cato*

Policy Report, and *Policy Analysis* articles such as "The American Welfare State: How We Spend Nearly $1 Trillion a Year Fighting Poverty—and Fail."

Center for American Progress
1333 H St. NW, 10th Floor, Washington, DC   20005
(202) 682-1611 • fax: (202) 682-1867
website: www.americanprogress.org

The Center for American Progress is a nonprofit, nonpartisan organization dedicated to improving the lives of Americans through progressive ideas and action. The center dialogues with leaders, thinkers, and citizens to explore the vital issues facing America and the world. The center publishes numerous research papers, which are available at its website, including, "The Right Choices to Cut Poverty and Restore Shared Prosperity."

Center for Law and Social Policy (CLASP)
1015 15th St. NW, Suite 400, Washington, DC   20005
(202) 906-8000 • fax: (202) 842-2885
e-mail: info@clasp.org
website: www.clasp.org

The Center for Law and Social Policy is a national nonprofit that works to improve the lives of low-income people. CLASP conducts research, provides policy analysis, advocates at the federal and state levels, and offers information and technical assistance on a range of family policy and equal justice issues. The center publishes many reports, briefs, and fact sheets, and also manages the website Spotlight on Poverty and Opportunity: The Source for News, Ideas, and Action, and initiative to help find solutions to economic hardship.

Center on Budget and Policy Priorities (CBPP)
820 First St. NE, Suite 510, Washington, DC   20002
(202) 408-1080 • fax: (202) 408-1056
e-mail: center@cbpp.org
website: www.cbpp.org

The Center on Budget and Policy Priorities is a policy organization working at the federal and state levels on fiscal policy and public programs that affect low- and moderate-income families and individuals. CBPP conducts research and analysis to inform public debates over proposed budget and tax policies, developing policy options to alleviate poverty. There are many reports available at CBPP's website, including "Social Security Keeps 20 Million Americans Out of Poverty: A State-By-State Analysis."

Children's Defense Fund (CDF)
25 E St. NW, Washington, DC   20001
(800) 233-1200
e-mail: cdfinfo@childrensdefense.org
website: www.childrensdefense.org

The Children's Defense Fund is a nonprofit child advocacy organization that works to ensure a level playing field for all American children, particularly poor and minority children, and those with disabilities. CDF champions policies and programs that lift children out of poverty, including the Head Start and Healthy Start programs. CDF publishes many reports, including the annual *State of America's Children*.

Coalition on Human Needs
1120 Connecticut Ave. NW, Suite 910, Washington, DC   20036
(202) 223-2532 • fax: (202) 223-2538
e-mail: info@chn.org
website: www.chn.org

The Coalition on Human Needs is an alliance of national organizations working together to promote public policies that address the needs of low-income and other vulnerable people. The coalition promotes adequate funding for human needs programs, progressive tax policies, and other federal measures to alleviate many of the problems confronted by low-income people. The organization publishes the *Human Needs Report* newsletter every other Friday when Congress is in session.

Economic Policy Institute (EPI)
1333 H St. NW, Suite 300, East Tower
Washington, DC   20005-4707
(202) 775-8810 • fax: (202) 775-0819
e-mail: researchdept@epi.org
website: www.epi.org

The Economic Policy Institute is a nonprofit, nonpartisan think tank that seeks to broaden the public debate about strategies to achieve a prosperous and fair economy. EPI conducts original research on economic issues, makes policy recommendations based on its findings, and disseminates its work to the appropriate audiences. Among the books, studies, issue briefs, popular education materials, and various other publications available are "Unions, Inequality, and Faltering Middle-Class Wages."

National Alliance to End Homelessness
1518 K St. NW, Suite 410, Washington, DC   20005
(202) 638-1526 • fax: (202) 638-4664
e-mail: naeh@naeh.org
website: www.endhomelessness.org

The National Alliance to End Homelessness is a nonpartisan organization committed to preventing and ending homelessness in the United States. The organization works collaboratively with the public, private, and nonprofit sectors to build stronger programs and policies that help communities achieve their goal of ending homelessness. The National Alliance to End Homelessness provides fact sheets, reports, presentations, briefs, and case studies at its website, including its annual *The State of Homelessness in America* report.

National Coalition for Homeless Veterans (NCHV)
333 ¹/₂ Pennsylvania Ave. SE, Washington, DC   20003
(800) VET-HELP • fax: (202) 546-2063
e-mail: info@nchv.org
website: www.nchv.org

The National Coalition for Homeless Veterans is a nonprofit organization that works to end homelessness among veterans by shaping public policy, promoting collaboration, and building the capacity of service providers. NCHV operates as a resource and technical assistance center for a national network of agencies that provide emergency and supportive housing, food, health services, job training and placement assistance, legal aid, and case management support for hundreds of thousands of homeless veterans each year. NCHV publishes information to provide assistance to community and faith-based organizations, government agencies, corporate partners, and the homeless veterans they serve.

National Coalition for the Homeless (NCH)
2201 P St. NW, Washington, DC   20037
(202) 462-4822 • fax: (202) 462-4823
e-mail: info@nationalhomeless.org
website: www.nationalhomeless.org

The National Coalition for the Homeless is a national network of homeless people, activists and advocates, community-based and faith-based service providers, and others committed to ending homelessness. NCH works to prevent and end homelessness while ensuring the immediate needs of those experiencing homelessness are met and their civil rights are protected. NCH publishes numerous reports and papers, available at their website, including "Hate Crimes Against the Homeless: Violence Hidden in Plain View."

National Law Center on Homelessness & Poverty
1411 K St. NW, Suite 1400, Washington, DC   20005
(202) 638-2535 • fax: (202) 628-2737
website: www.nlchp.org

The National Law Center on Homelessness & Poverty works to prevent and end homelessness by serving as the legal arm of the nationwide movement to end homelessness in America. The organization pursues this mission through impact litigation, policy advocacy, and public education. The center publishes a monthly newsletter, *In Just Times*, as well as periodic reports, including "'Simply Unacceptable': Homelessness and the Human Right to Housing in the United States 2011."

Urban Institute
2100 M St. NW, Washington, DC   20037
(202) 833-7200
website: www.urban.org

The Urban Institute works to foster sound public policy and effective government by gathering data, conducting research, evaluating programs, and educating Americans on social and economic issues. The Urban Institute builds knowledge about the nation's social and fiscal challenges through evidence-based research meant to diagnose problems and figure out which policies and programs work best, for whom, and how. The Urban Institute publishes policy briefs, commentary, and research reports, including "Poverty in the United States."

Bibliography

Books

Xavier de Souza Briggs, Susan J. Popkin, and John Goering	*Moving to Opportunity: The Story of an American Experiment to Fight Ghetto Poverty.* New York: Oxford University Press, 2010.
Christian Broda and David E. Weinstein	*Prices, Poverty, and Inequality: Why Americans Are Better Off than You Think.* Washington, DC: AEI Press, 2008.
Nicholas N. Eberstadt	*The Poverty of "The Poverty Rate": Measure and Mismeasure of Want in Modern America.* Washington, DC: AEI Press, 2008.
Peter Edelman	*So Rich, So Poor: Why It's So Hard to End Poverty in America.* New York: New Press, 2012.
Ingrid Gould Ellen and Brendan O'Flaherty, eds.	*How to House the Homeless.* New York: Russell Sage Foundation, 2010.
Kevin Fitzpatrick and Mark LaGory	*Unhealthy Cities: Poverty, Race, and Place in America.* New York: Routledge, 2011.
Alyosha Goldstein	*Poverty in Common: The Politics of Community Action During the American Century.* Durham, NC: Duke University Press, 2012.

Ron Haskins and
Isabel Sawhill

Creating an Opportunity Society.
Washington, DC: Brookings
Institution Press, 2009.

Ella Howard

*Homeless: Poverty and Place in Urban
America.* Philadelphia, PA: University
of Pennsylvania Press, 2013.

Woody Klein

*American Poverty: Presidential
Failures and a Call to Action.*
Washington, DC: Potomac Books,
2013.

Stephen Pimpare

*A People's History of Poverty in
America.* New York: New Press, 2008.

Edward Royce

*Poverty and Power: The Problem of
Structural Inequality.* New York:
Rowman & Littlefield, 2008.

Kevin Ryan and
Tina Kelley

*Almost Home: Helping Kids Move
from Homelessness to Hope.* Hoboken,
NJ: Wiley, 2012.

Russell K. Schutt
and Stephen M.
Goldfinger

*Homelessness, Housing, and Mental
Illness.* Cambridge, MA: Harvard
University Press, 2011.

Tavis Smiley and
Cornel West

*The Rich and the Rest of Us: A
Poverty Manifesto.* New York: Smiley
Books, 2012.

Jason Adam
Wasserman and
Jeffrey Michael
Clair

*At Home on the Street: People,
Poverty, and a Hidden Culture of
Homelessness.* Boulder, CO: Lynne
Rienner Publishers, 2010.

Periodicals and Internet Sources

America	"Homeless Soldiers," November 15, 2010. http://americamagazine.org.
Michael Barone	"Personal Well-Being Overshadows Income Inequality," *Washington Examiner*, January 2, 2011.
Melissa Boteach	"5 Things You Need to Know About the 2001 Poverty Data," Center for American Progress, September 12, 2012. www.americanprogress.org.
Children's Defense Fund	"Child Poverty in America: 2011," September 2012. www.childrensdefense.org.
Coalition on Human Needs	"The Recession Generation: Preventing Long-Term Damage from Child Poverty and Young Adult Joblessness," July 2010. www.chn.org.
John Diaz	"The Issue That Won't Go Away," *San Francisco Chronicle*, June 10, 2012.
Shaun Donovan	"Ending Homelessness in Our Time: Why Smart Government Is Key," *Public Manager*, Winter 2011.
James A. Dorn	"Poor Choices," *Baltimore Sun*, September 27, 2011.
Nicholas Eberstadt	"Are Entitlements Corrupting Us? Yes, American Character Is at Stake," *Wall Street Journal*, September 1, 2012.

Nicholas
Eberstadt

"A Poverty of Statistics," *The American*, September 18, 2010. www.american.com.

Barbara
Ehrenreich

"Why Homelessness Is Becoming an Occupy Wall Street Issue," *Mother Jones*, October 24, 2011. www.motherjones.com.

Rana Foroohar

"The Truth About the Poverty Crisis," *Time*, September 26, 2011.

Shawn Fremstad

"Married . . . Without Means: Poverty and Economic Hardship Among Married Americans," Center for Economic and Policy Research, November 2012. www.cepr.net.

Tana Ganeva

"We're a Country That Lets Kids Go Homeless," *AlterNet*, July 16, 2012. www.alternet.org.

Jonah Goldberg

"In a Welfare State, How Much Is 'Enough'?," *National Review Online*, June 2, 2010. www.nationalreview .com.

Elizabeth Grayer
and Gwen Moore

"Families Still Need Safety Net," *Politico*, April 21, 2011. www.politico.com.

Bob Herbert

"Raising False Alarms," *New York Times*, January 25, 2011.

Hank Kalet

"Evicting the Homeless: Civil Rights for Homeless Communities Wane Across the Country," *In These Times*, July 31, 2012. www.inthesetimes.com.

Gary E.
MacDougal

"The Wrong Way to Help the Poor,"
New York Times, October 11, 2012.

Courtney Martin

"Homelessness Is Not Just About
Housing," *American Prospect*, May 1,
2011. www.prospect.org.

Aparna Mathur
and Michael R.
Strain

"Are Minimum Wages Fair?" *Blaze*,
July 18, 2012. www.theblaze.com.

Allan H. Meltzer

"A Welfare State or a Start-up
Nation?" *Wall Street Journal*, June 15,
2011.

Charles Murray

"The New American Divide," *Wall
Street Journal*, January 23, 2012.

Robert Rector

"Marriage: America's Greatest
Weapon Against Child Poverty,"
Heritage Foundation Special Report,
September 5, 2012. www.heritage.org.

Amy Roden

"No Way to Help the Poor," *The
American*, January 5, 2010.
www.american.com.

John Schmitt

"The Minimum Wage Is Too Damn
Low," *Issue Brief*, Center for
Economic and Policy Research,
March 2012. www.cepr.net.

Nick Schulz

"Raising Minimum Wage Is
Maximum Stupidity," *Boston Herald*,
April 11, 2012.

Eliot Spitzer

"Young, Poor, and Desperate," *Slate*,
September 19, 2011. www.slate.com.

Michael Tanner · "Obama Encouraging Americans to Get on Welfare," Politico.com, July 18, 2012. www.politico.com.

Paul N. Van de Water and Arloc Sherman · "Social Security Keeps 20 Million Americans Out of Poverty: A State-by-State Analysis," Center on Budget and Policy Priorities, August 11, 2010. www.cbpp.org.

Mark Weisbrot · "Minimum Wage Raise Is the Least We Can Do to Civilize America," McClatchy Tribune Information Services, August 28, 2012.

Index

A

Affordable Care Act, 130
Afghanistan, 89, 152
African Americans, 33, 112–113
After-tax income, 53
Age and poverty rates, 23–24
Aid to Families with Dependent Children (AFDC), 67, 88
Air-conditioning in poor households, 48–49, 54–55
American Enterprise Institute, 118
American Recovery and Reinvestment Act (ARRA) (2009), 65–66, 71, 82
Annual Homeless Assessment Report (AHAR), 150
Anti-poverty programs
    accurate information for, 63
    employment and, 132
    impact of spending on, 95, 96
    investment in, 75, 97–99
    success of, 57
    variety of, 88–92
    See also Federal low-income housing programs; specific programs
Asian Americans, 112–113
Automobile ownership, 52, 60

B

Baby Boomers, 102
Bachmann, Michele, 86
Baker, Mary Kay, 104–105
Bandow, Doug, 180–183
Battistoni, Alyssa, 109

Bergh, Andreas, 101
Biggs, Andrew G., 100–103
Birth control access, 143
Blank, Rebecca M., 17
Bloomberg, Michael, 185
Bloomberg View, 56–58
Boskin Commission, 50
Boston Globe (newspaper), 185
Bottom quartile individuals, 38
Bottom-quintile individuals, 54–55
Brookings Institution, 101, 125
Brooks, Arthur, 103, 138
Buffett, Warren, 124
Bureau of Labor Statistics, 18
Burt, Martha, 161
Bush, George H. W., 131
Bush, George W., 42, 92, 155, 166

C

Cancer breakthroughs, 33
Capacity Building for Sustainable Communities Fund, 90
Capitalism, 134–140
Capitalism and Freedom (Friedman), 137
Cato Institute, 43
Center for American Progress, 18
Center for Budget and Policy Priorities, 41, 42
Center for Effective Government, 43
Child poverty rates, 22, 23–24, 115, 133
    See also Young families with children

Markee, Patrick, 39–46
Marriage
    benefits of marriage, 143–144
    birth control access, 143
    births outside marriage, 141–142
    is not solution against poverty, 145–148
    is solution against poverty, 141–144
    two-caste system, 142–143
Marriage and Caste in America: Separate and Unequal Families in a Post-Marital Age (Hymowitz), 144
Martin, Paul, 185–186
Material well-being, 48–49, 52–53
McKenzie, Richard, 96
McKinney-Vento homeless assistance programs, 161, 174, 177
Medicaid
    beneficiaries, 91, 175
    cuts to, 34
    expenditures on, 92–93
    impact of, 17, 130
    improvements needed, 178
    as income benefits, 56
    size of, 91, 130
Medicare
    Baby Boomers and, 102
    cuts to, 34
    government support of, 91
    as income benefits, 56
    tax breaks, 86
Mentally disabled persons, 153, 175
Messmore, Ryan, 105
Mexico, 32
Meyer, Bruce D., 47–55, 57, 72–73
Microwaves in poor households, 60

Millennial Housing Commission, 177
Minimum wage
    economic downturn and, 117–118
    economic growth and, 115–116
    economic stimulus effect of, 116–117
    families affected by, 114–115
    raising would help workers, 111–118
    worker demographics, 111–114
Money income measure, 29
Moses, Joy, 145–148
Moynihan, Patrick, 37
Murray, Charles, 134–140

N

National Academy of Sciences (NAS), 52, 82
National Alliance to End Homelessness, 152, 154, 159, 171–179
National Center for Children in Poverty (NCCP), 18
National Coalition for the Homeless, 41, 45
National Housing Trust Fund, 44, 162
National Low Income Housing Coalition, 44
National Public Radio, 47
Nativity and poverty rates, 24
Neighborhood Planning Grants, 90
New England Journal of Medicine (magazine), 150

New Freedom Commission on
Mental Health, 177
New York Times (newspaper), 40,
118, 185
Noncash welfare benefits, 95
Non-Hispanic white workers, 112
Northeast Ohio Coalition for the
Homeless, 40, 42
Norway, 32

O

Obama, Barack (administration),
45, 86, 89
anti-poverty programs, 89, 92
economic disparity, 123
free enterprise, 102
government spending, 100
social finance, 185
Occupational Safety and Health
Administration, 139
Occupy Wall Street, 40–41, 46
OMB Watch, 43
Organization for Economic Coop-
eration and Development
(OECD), 31–32
Orren, Gary, 127
Orshansky, Mollie, 73
Orszag, Peter, 58

P

Page, Benjamin, 127
Pathways to Housing, 156
Patient Protection and Affordable
Care Act, 95
Pell Grants, 91, 98
Permanent supportive housing,
171–179
Personal computers, 60

Personal Responsibility and Work
Responsibility Act (1996), 95,
108
Poverty
approaches to solving, 145–
147
consumption data and, 50–52
as death sentence, 32–34
decline in, 47–55
housing affordability crisis,
61–62
income deficit or surplus, 26,
28
income-to-poverty ratio, 26,
27–28
introduction, 16–19
living standard, improve-
ments, 54–55
marriage and, 141–144
material well-being, 48–49,
52–53
not serious problem, 59–63
official measures of, 47–48
overview, 21–30, 126
problem with analyses over,
49–50
shared households, 28–30
social assistance and, 88–99
stabilizers, 58
state of, 129–133
See also Anti-poverty programs; Young families with
children
The Poverty of the Poverty Rate
(Eberstadt), 126
Poverty rates
accurate information needed,
62–63
child poverty rates, 22, 23–24,
115, 133
extent of, 82–83

current approach problems, 97–98
impact on poverty rate, 95–96
poverty reduction and, 88–99
recession impact on, 93–95
variety of programs, 88–90
welfare spending increases, 92–93
Social financing for homeless, 184–186
Social Security
  attacks on, 86–87
  Baby Boomers and, 102
  cuts to, 34
  government support of, 91, 92
  poverty rate and, 16, 75
  poverty reduction and, 57, 84–87
  as safe investment, 85–86
  success of, 84–85
Social Security Administration, 84–85
Soros, George, 136
State Children's Health Insurance Program, 91
Stiglitz, Joseph E., 119–122
Stimulus bill, 74, 94, 161
Substance Abuse and Mental Health Services Administration (SAMHSA), 151
Sullivan, James X., 47–55, 57, 72–73
Sum, Andrew M., 35–38
Supplemental Nutrition Assistance Program (SNAP)
  economic conditions of participants, 68–69
  effects of, 18
  overview, 65
  recession impact, 69–70
  recipient characteristics, 66–68

recipient increase of, 65–66
spending increase for, 70–71
Supplemental Poverty Measure (SPM), 18–19, 30
Supplemental Security Income (SSI), 16, 67, 91
Survivor benefits, 16
Sweden, 32, 62, 127
Switzerland, 32

T

Take Back the Land, 40
Tanner, Michael, 88–99
Tax credits, 56–57, 82
Tax deductions, 17
Tax reform, 73–75
Tea Party movement, 44, 86
Temporary Assistance for Needy Families (TANF), 67, 88, 93, 131–132
Temporary homelessness, 61, 62–63
Ten Year Plans to End Homelessness, 174
Thompson, Derek, 187–190
Transitional housing programs, 160
Trickle-down economics, 120–121
Turkey, 32
Two-caste system, 142–143

U

Unemployment, 68–70
Unemployment benefits, 82
University of Chicago, 72
University of Notre Dame, 72
University of Pennsylvania, 155–156